Thinking Literature

Anna Kwiatek   Marcelina Połczyńska
Agnieszka Romanowska   Wiktoria Wawrzyńczyk

Thinking Literature

Essays on reading
literary classics
today

Jagiellonian University Press

REVIEW
Prof. dr hab. Jean Ward

COVER DESIGN
Marta Jaszczuk

On the cover: Mabel May Woodward, *Afternoon respite*

This publication was funded by the Faculty of Philology at the Jagiellonian University

© Copyright by Jagiellonian University – Jagiellonian University Press
 First edition, Kraków 2024
 All rights reserved

This publication is protected by the Polish Act on Copyright and Related Rights. The Publisher, Jagiellonian University Press and other entitled authors, creators, entities are the copyright holders. Copying, distributing and other use of this publication in full or in part without the Publisher's consent is prohibited except for permitted personal and public use or under an open access license granted by the Publisher.

ISBN 978-83-233-5407-9 (print)
ISBN 978-83-233-7588-3 (PDF)
ISBN 978-83-233-7589-0 (epub)
https://doi.org/10.4467/K7588.18/24.24.19675

www.wuj.pl

Jagiellonian University Press
Editorial Offices: Michałowskiego 9/2, 31-126 Kraków
Phone: +48 12 663 23 80
Distribution: Phone: +48 12 631 01 97
Cell Phone: +48 506 006 674, e-mail: sprzedaz@wuj.pl
Bank: PEKAO SA, IBAN PL 80 1240 4722 1111 0000 4856 3325

Contents

Preface VII

MARCELINA POŁCZYŃSKA
1. "These Currents of History": Kinship, Fidelity, the
State and (Its) Violence in *Antigone* and *Home Fire* 1

WIKTORIA WAWRZYŃCZYK
2. Stitches and Stories:
Ahmed Saadawi's *Frankenstein in Baghdad* 33

ANNA KWIATEK
3. "Twixt my extremes and me this bloody knife / Shall
play the umpire": Suicide (Not) Romanticised in *Romeo
and Juliet* and *Hamlet* 59

AGNIESZKA ROMANOWSKA
4. *Hag-Seed* by Margaret Atwood as a Meta-artistic
Exploration of William Shakespeare's *The Tempest* 93

Index 125

Preface

In her chapter for *The Cambridge Companion to "Frankenstein,"* Lisa Vargo observes that

> the assemblage of textual sources employed by Mary Shelley provides a testament to the importance of reading, a key aspect of a programme of personal and social improvement she shared with her father William Godwin and practised throughout her life. (...) Her dedication of the novel to [Godwin] suggests that in its most ideal form, reading is for Mary Shelley a communal activity, and reminds us that our own engagements with reading, such as in classes and book clubs, are models for sociability that are deeply important.[1]

Referring to Godwin's views, expressed in his *Enquiry Concerning Political Justice*, on the importance of freedom of social communication,

---

[1] Vargo, Lisa. 2016. "Contextualizing Sources." In: *The Cambridge Companion to Frankenstein*. Ed. Andrew Smith. Cambridge. Cambridge University Press, pp. 26–32 (26–28).

conversation and sharing ideas, Vargo discusses *Frankenstein* as a work which thematises Mary Shelley's conviction that "reading involves a sense of dialogue with individuals and with one's society."[2] Inspired by this perception of reading, the title of the present volume, "thinking literature," is meant to indicate interpreting the world around us through and with the help of literature, reading in order to think and share our thoughts with others, and using literature as a tool to contemplate human condition against the background of the past and in connection with the present.

Interactions with literary classics discussed in this book demonstrate one of the ways in which reading can be a socially significant communal activity. Ancient tragedy, Shakespeare, and Mary Shelley's novel are read anew and applied to the challenges and dangers of the contemporary world. This process of thinking literature in the minds of rewriters, adaptors and interpreters is then shared with others, readers and audiences, thus creating the sense of dialogue without which the social aspect of reading would not be fulfilled. The idea to create the present volume originated in my literature classes in which canonical texts are discussed year after year with new generations of students. It has its source in an environment particularly supportive of reading practised as a communal activity. Where, if not in universities, can Godwin's freedom of social communication flourish to the benefit of those who, unlike Mary Shelley's protagonists, may be spared the risks of "neglected and selective"[3] reading? In this context an important quality of this book is that three of its authors are young readers and budding literary scholars.

The first essay discusses Kamila Shamsie's 2017 novel *Home Fire*, a contemporary retelling of *Antigone* by Sophocles, which transplants

---

[2] Ibid., p. 28.

[3] Ibid., p. 31.

the ancient conflict over burial rights and the legitimacy of law to the community of British Muslims in contemporary London. Marcelina Połczyńska's comparative reading of *Antigone* and *Home Fire*, informed by Judith Butler's views on the relationship between kinship and the state and Giorgio Agamben's theory of *homo sacer* and state of exception, focuses on the nature of law and sovereignty, the issue of fidelity of and to the state, and an individual's engagement with politics in the context of the increasing employment of citizenship deprivation powers in the UK and the consequent othering of the British Muslim community.

In the second chapter of the book Wiktoria Wawrzyńczyk examines Ahmed Saadawi's *Frankenstein in Baghdad* to identify fragmentation as the novel's key device. Inspired by Mary Shelley's protagonist, whose body consists of assembled fragments stitched together by the ambitious but irresponsible scientist, the novelist uses fragmentation on many levels of his 2013 novel. From the nonlinear plot, multiple points of view, mixture of real, surreal and supernatural occurrences, to the massacred bodies of the victims and shattered biographies of the survivors – the novel reflects the atrocities of violence in post-2003 Iraq. In her conclusion, the author observes that the social commitment of Saadawi's novel is not limited to the immediate context of the novel's setting but pertains to a number of acute problems and crises we are facing nowadays on a global scale. Saadawi's book reflects very similar concerns about the condition and future of humankind to those that Mary Shelley shared with her readers when she was writing her cautionary tale about Victor Frankenstein.

The third essay deals with the issue of suicide in Shakespeare's plays, one of the difficult themes that are being commented on, especially on the web, as potentially dangerous or harmful to vulnerable audiences. Taking as her starting point the existing popular discussion on the sensitive content in Shakespeare, Anna Kwiatek offers an analysis of *Romeo and Juliet* and *Hamlet* in order to inspect the concerns voiced against Shakespeare allegedly romanticising suicidal death in his plays. She argues that although there are moments in the plays in which suicide is elevated, they have to be viewed and interpreted within an integrated framework of the internal logic of each play, including its rhetorical features and epoch-specific conventions. This chapter confirms the unceasing topicality of the discussion on how the reception of an author so ubiquitously present in education and theatre as Shakespeare is shaped by our changing sensitivities and concerns.

In the last chapter Margaret Atwood's 2016 novel *Hag-Seed*, a retelling of *The Tempest*, is discussed as an extended meta-artistic game played with Shakespeare. I analyse Atwood's imaginative and multifaceted dialogue with Shakespeare's play to argue that it takes the form of a dense and intricate web of meta-artistic interactions performed on various levels of the novel. From the structure of the para-texts, wordplays on the characters' names, and the symbolic timeframe, to the novel's meta-theatricality and focus on language, to the concern with the position of the artist, the significance of artistic creation, and the potentially healing power of art, the novelist's thinking Shakespeare is inventive and convincing.

Philip Smith called Atwood's retelling a meditation on modern readers' relationship with Shakespeare and an attempt to understand their contemporary experiences through the playwright's *oeuvre*.[4] The same can be said about the other instances of thinking literature presented in this volume. The four essays testify to the lasting relevance of works of literature created in previous epochs, the significance of

---

[4] Smith, Philip. 2017. "Margaret Atwood's Tempests: Critique of Shakespearean Essentialism in *Bodily Harm* and *Hag-Seed*." *Margaret Atwood Studies* 11 (2017), 29–40 (30).

their cultural legacy and the impressive scope of their impact. The contemporary interactions with ancient Greek tragedy, Shakespeare and *Frankenstein* discussed here are examples of reading as a communal activity. Thinking literature by revisiting canonical texts and sharing with others the experience this brings, helps us to define, understand and confront the social and political challenges of today's increasingly complex world.

Agnieszka Romanowska

MARCELINA POŁCZYŃSKA

1.
"These Currents of History": Kinship, Fidelity, the State and (Its) Violence in *Antigone* and *Home Fire*

Introduction

In a 2022 article published in *The Guardian* on the Conservative policy of the hostile environment, Kamila Shamsie wrote that "surely the minimum we should be able to expect of our government is an acknowledgement of human dignity" (Shamsie 2022). Yet her 2017 novel, *Home Fire*, critically examines just how fraught something as fundamental as human rights and universal dignity has become in the eyes of British lawmakers and politicians in the wake of the "war on terror." The novel is a retelling of *Antigone* that transplants the original conflict over burial rights and the legitimacy of law from ancient Thebes to modern London. As such, it joins a long tradition of adapting Sophocles' play to the contemporary socio-political circumstances (Weiss 2022). Simultaneously, it stands in opposition to the newer corpora of post-9/11 literature that focuses on the perspective of the returning veteran and constitutes an attempt at "wresting victimhood from the invader and reframing the war as a needlessly violent fiasco" (Krause 2020, 15). However, what both *Home Fire* and *Antigone* dissect and examine is not just the reality of war, but the forces and interests that inscribe violence into law. The forces that enable the excess of violence and that lead to the state of exception – a circumstance, as delineated by Giorgio Agamben, in which lies the state's power to deprive individuals of citizenship and turn them into *homo sacer* – that is, turn them into an ungrieveable loss.

The focal point of *Antigone* is the issue of burial rites. With two brothers dying during their power struggle for the rule over Thebes, the divine law requires that they both be buried – for if they are not, their souls will not be able to cross to the netherworld. Creon, the maternal uncle of the brothers and the newly crowned king of Thebes, rules that only Eteocles is to be buried. He deems Polynices, the usurper who attacked the city in the hope of overthrowing his brother, as unworthy to lie in the ground soiled by his treason. Creon believes that loyalty to the state – and thus to him, as its king and embodiment – is paramount: "Never to grant traitors and subversives equal footing with loyal citizens, but to honour patriots in life and death" (Heaney 2004, 11).[1] Antigone, the sister of

---

[1] Though not favoured by classicists, for the purposes of this text, I shall refer to Seamus Heaney's 2004 *Antigone* translation, *The Burial at Thebes*, for two main reasons: firstly, it is one of the two translations Kamila Shamsie used while writing *Home Fire* (Shamsie 2018a), the other one being by Anne Carson; secondly, due to Heaney's conscious referencing of the post-9/11 "war on terror" context in the translation (Meltzer 2011; Weiss 2022) – a perspective particularly pertinent for Shamsie's reimaging of the play.

both Polynices and Eteocles, believes it unethical not to bury Polynices. She sees her obligation arising from kinship as of greater paramountcy than the binding law of Creon's edict. Having failed to entice the support of her sister, Ismene, Antigone buries Polynices alone just outside Thebes. An important and somewhat perplexing element of the plot is that Antigone performs the burial rites twice and is only captured the second time around. When she is caught and brought before Creon, despite having pronounced the death penalty for anyone who dares to bury Polynices, he does not order her execution. Instead, she is to be walled in and given just enough food to stay alive.

Having disavowed Ismene for her refusal to join her in open defiance of Creon and his edict, Antigone sees herself as a living dead, content to see her tomb as her wedding chamber. Though Haemon, Creon's son and Antigone's betrothed, pleads with his father to see the error of his ways, it is not until Tiresias, the blind prophet, confronts him with the vision of the calamitous consequences of his actions that Creon relents and arranges for the burial of Polynices. A change of heart, however, that comes too late. With Antigone having hanged herself in her tomb, the grief-stricken Haemon, in turn, kills himself, which pushes his mother to take her own life as well when she hears of his suicide. As the sun sets on the carnage of human pride, the Chorus sings: "those who overbear will be brought to grief. Fate will flail them on its winnowing floor and in due season teach them to be wise" (Heaney 2004, 56). The final scene sees Creon being led back to the palace, remaining the king of the city, hollowed out by the price of his fidelity to the state and to what he believed to be right.

The continuous presence of the play in Western cultural and philosophical consciousness is manifest in the ongoing preoccupation with the question of the political character of the play and its titular character. Though many a reading and theory have been produced, none seems as pertinent to the modern reader of the play as the one proposed by Judith Butler.

Butler's claim – *Antigone* as the queering of kinship and gender

In *Antigone's Claim*, Judith Butler builds their argumentation in dialogue and opposition to the established interpretations by Hegel and Lacan. Namely, they disagree with the Hegelian assumption, later to a certain extent echoed by Lacan, of separability of kinship and the social. As Butler notes,

> for Lacan, kinship is rarefied as enabling linguistic structure, a presupposition of symbolic intelligibility, and thus removed from the domain of the social; for Hegel, kinship is precisely a relation of "blood" rather than one of norms. That is, kinship is not yet entered into the social, where the social is inaugurated through supersession of kinship. (Butler 2000, 3)

The understanding of kinship as a social construct is expedient for understanding the character of Antigone as a political agent – notably, a dimension of her character rejected by both the Hegelian and Lacanian readings. Fundamental to the Hegelian dialectic is the binary opposition he places Antigone and Creon in. He sees Antigone as the universal embodiment of the prepolitical morality, and thus, one that lacks ethical consciousness and agency. Hegel understands the play to be a clash of symmetrically antithetical claims – for only such a clash can propel change (Robert 2010; Meltzer 2011). Conversely, Lacan's understanding of Antigone as being impelled into her act of defiance by pure desire, "a motivation without motive," divorces her from consciously engaging in any dialectic with Creon. To Lacan, it is precisely this lack of dialogue that makes her act ethical, but it leads the play to a place "where language rebounds in a self-referential echoing with no connection to social or political debate" (Leonard 2006, 128–129). It is precisely due to this disengagement with the social and disinterest in how Antigone's agency and consciousness inform her actions that I will not refer much to the Hegelian and Lacanian lines of thought in respect to the Sophoclean play. As I am not a classicist, my choice to focus on Butler's understanding of the text is motivated not by any intrinsic judgement as to the merit of each analysis of the original play, but rather by the merit of juxtaposing Butler's analysis with Shamsie's reimagination of the text.

It is the complex interplay between kinship and the state that is of particular interest to Butler. For them, kinship and the state exist not in opposition, but as mutually informing and validating entities, i.e. one cannot exist without the other:

> Not only does the state presuppose kinship and kinship presuppose the state but "acts" that are performed in the name of the one principle take place in the idiom of the other, confounding the distinction between the two at a rhetorical level and thus bringing into crisis the stability of the conceptual distinction between them. (Butler 2000, 11–12)

This problematises the traditional opposition of Antigone and Creon, for neither of them can clearly represent either kinship or the state. As Butler argues, the incestuous character of Antigone's familial relationships queers any act of kinship she engages in. What's more, the firmness she exhibits through her act of defiance in the name of sororal, albeit preposterous, love leads also to the queering of her gender, for this firmness, imbued with masculinity, impugns the fundamental kinship that informs the distinction between genders. Furthermore, Creon's claim to sovereignty, thus his claim to represent the state, is based on kinship. He ascends to the throne for he is the only viable successor left in the Theban royal family.

Butler's analysis problematises not only the relationality of kinship to the state, but also highlights Antigone's own contingent relationship with kinship. The opening scene of the play portrays the failure of solidarity between Antigone and Ismene, for the latter sister refuses to openly defy Creon's edict – a betrayal that essentially renders her dead to Antigone. However, as Butler (similarly to most scholars) pays little attention both to the character of Ismene and the implication of the disintegration of that sisterhood, I will return to this aspect of Antigone's problematic conception of kinship later. The more widely considered instance of Antigone's strained relationality with kinship comes with her final speech, where she proclaims that

> not for a husband, not even for a son would [she] have broken the law. Another husband [she] could always find and have other sons by him if one were lost. But with [her] father gone, and [her] mother gone, where can [she] find another brother, ever? (Heaney 2004, 40)

Some, such as Goethe, H.D.F. Kitto, and R.C. Jebb, view the speech as too cold and calculated to be considered authentic, seeing it rather as a later addition (Honig 2010, 10). Bonnie Honig, however, sees it as a deliberately offensive speech – one which through citing incongruous and cruel reasoning indicates "the politics, promise, and violence of reason giving itself" (2010, 11). She further suggests that this proclamation of unique singularity of Polynices could be critically engaging with the ideas that were pronounced a few years later, although pertinent to public discourse for some time by then, in Pericles' Funeral Oration. The speech appealed to parents of still childbearing age to forego prolonged mourning over their dead sons and to instead procreate and replace them with new children (Honig 2010, 11–12).

On intratextual level, within her offensive speech, Antigone usurps the masculine position that assumes the replicability of women expressed earlier in the text by Creon. When Ismene beseeches him to reconsider Antigone's punishment as he would be depriving Haemon, his son, of his betrothed, Creon replies: "He has other fields to plough" (Heaney 2004, 27). The subversion and deconstruction of kinship verbalised within this speech affirms a critical engagement with the pathologization of kinship for the purposes and interests of the state. As Butler argues, it is not in consequence of breaching the incest taboo that the family is decimated, but in consequence of the state's enlistment of the family "in the service of its own militarization" (Butler 2000, 36). However, the speech also "represents [Antigone's] rejection of normative patriarchal structures" (Leonard 2006, 130). Antigone queers kinship by prioritising a form of it that leaves her neither a mother, nor a wife, thus useless to patriarchy. This queering further emphasises just how much the state depends on the adherence to the heteronormative forms of kinship to retain the status quo, and therefore, power.

Interestingly, however, the Sophoclean *Antigone* was written in the time of and, as Honig argues, in response to invested engagement of the state in the changing of the status quo – "a shift from an aristocratic ethics and politics of individuality and distinction to a democratic ethics and politics of interchangeability" (2009, 13). Antigone's claim of Polynices's irreplaceability echoes this affirmation of the irreducible individuality that Solon, through his reforms on funerary practices, aimed to stifle. These reforms were introduced partly to put an end to cycles of acts of vengeance, and partly to reframe mourning as an honouring of the life of the deceased and their contributions to the polis, rather than excessive lamentation expressing a sense of irredeemable loss (Honig 2009, 11–12). Crucially, however, they prohibited the traditional inclusion of keening, which by then would be performed by professional female mourners "from whom mourning was a central activity" and "who knew best how to move people in their grief" (Honig 2009, 21). This further recontextualises the perceived offensiveness of Antigone's speech. By employing the callous logic-based argumentation, she also refrains from keening when expressing her grief in public, destabilising the expression of her gender even further.

The assertion that Creon, in this light, would represent democratic order might seem counterintuitive, given the excessive nature of the punishment imposed posthumously on Polynices for his treason. After all, Creon decreed not just to cast Polynices's corpse outside of the city limits (a standard Attic punishment at that time), but to leave the body exposed so that it would rot (Honig 2009, 9). The portrayal of Creon as a democrat, albeit one who exercises the power invested in him with a heavy hand, can also seem unfounded because of the contemporary reclamation of Antigone as a democratic agent of civil disobedience (Wiltshire 1976). However, such thinking miscasts the issue of excessive power as arising from state ideology that purports excess, rather than a state apparatus that allows it. The particular ideological alliance informing Creon's reign is secondary to his inability to heed advice and consider the long-term repercussions of his excess. He fails both on the individual level, as he is to lose all his family by the time the sun sets, and on the communal, as by leaving Polynices's corpse exposed he risks pollution spreading across the whole city. Creon is not bereft of good intentions. His tragic fault is his inflexibility, his obstinacy – a fault he shares with Antigone, who, rather than being his opposite, is really his foil. The difference between them, much rather than the disposition of true wisdom and true foolishness as Rosanna Lauriola (2007) has argued, is access to power. Though Antigone at various points throughout the play appropriates the voice of authority, unlike Creon, she does not possess it. Thus, the excess of her speech act does not disperse into an excess of enforcement. That Creon seems blind to Antigone not being an opponent of equal footing is the true mark of his villainy.

To return to Butler – one of the key assertions they make in *Antigone's Claim* in regard to kinship and the state is not only that Antigone's claim betrays their complex interdependence, but that her claim and its circumstances allegorise the crisis of kinship. As put by Butler, this crisis pertains to the legitimacy of loss – it begs the question "which social arrangements can be recognised as legitimate loves, and which human losses can be explicitly grieved as real and consequential loss?" (Butler 2000, 24). The disruptive character of Antigone's dissent betrays the ontological entanglement of kinship and the state, in the wake of which the crisis of one generates the crisis of the other. Butler argues that kinship, just like gender, is performative, i.e. its material existence is achieved through recurrent exercise of a set of practices and affirming actions. Therefore, it is not only that Antigone's defiance arises from her sense of kinship, but that it reaffirms it. Against the narrative of the state, she claims that Polynices should be recognised as kin – a "performative repetition that reinstates kinship as a public scandal" (Butler 2000, 57–58). This notion of the scandalising effect that such a proclamation can have directly ties in with Butler's assertion that Antigone's grief is for an ungrieveable loss. Drawing comparisons to the predicament of the AIDS epidemic and its double tragedy of loss unaccounted for and grief unrecognised, to Butler, Antigone refuses the law for the law refuses her loss. Therefore, she epitomises the expression and experience of "[grieving] within the presumption of criminality" (Butler 2000, 78). To understand better the concept of the ungrieveable loss and the circumstances that both originate and necessitate it, I would like to briefly turn to the work of Giorgio Agamben regarding *homo sacer* and the state of exception.

"A space devoid of law" – *homo sacer* and the state of exception

The concept of *homo sacer*, upon which Agamben builds his theory of bare life and the state of exception that inaugurates it, derives from Roman criminal law and is seen by some as "[the law's] oldest punishment" (Bennet qtd. in Agamben 1998, 71). However, the contradictory nature of the concept complicates such a perspective and betrays the inherent entanglement of the state's relationship to life.

The antithetical essence of *homo sacer* arises from the fact that he is excluded from sacrifice, yet he can be killed without punishment by anyone. Violence enacted against him is thus no longer recognisable as violence; no longer a citizen – a life with rights – he becomes bare life (Agamben 1998, 81–83). It is important to note that Agamben argues that each society decides on "a threshold beyond which life ceases to have any juridical value and can, therefore, be killed without the commission of a homicide" (1998, 139). It is the establishing of that threshold that enacts "the production of bare life [which constitutes] the originary activity of sovereignty" (Agamben 1998, 83). Moreover, the sacred man as the embodiment of bare life remains in a unique relationality to the sovereign, for it is this "continuous relationship to power" that maintains his banishment and reinstitutes the lack of the law's applicability to him, making his the most political existence (Agamben 1998, 183–184). Crucial for the consideration of the current political condition of the West is the recognition of the markedly and increasingly biopolitical reconfiguration of that threshold where one can kill without committing murder. "[In] the age of biopolitics," the power of setting that threshold has transformed into the authority that sets the political relevance of life:

> When life becomes the supreme political value, not only is the problem of life's nonvalue thereby posed, as Schmitt suggests but further, it is as if the ultimate ground of sovereign power were at stake in this decision. In modern biopolitics, sovereign is he who decides on the value or the nonvalue of life as such. Life – which, with the declarations of rights, had as such been invested with the principle of sovereignty – now itself becomes the place of a sovereign decision. (Agamben 1998, 142)

This transformation has been possible as the concept of bare life and the power invested with the capacity to pronounce it became disengaged from the state of exception.

The state of exception presents itself as another intrinsically paradoxical concept, for it constitutes the employment of the suspension of the law as a juridical device that reinstates the state's sovereignty. As such, it is of interest to Agamben in its capacity to act as the foundational ground for any conceptualisation of the relationship that simultaneously confines and deserts life within law. The modern application of the state of exception originates from the institution of the state of siege. It was introduced in the French Constituent Assembly's decree of July 8, 1791, and allowed for the passing of all powers bestowed on the civil authority to maintain order and police the public to the military commander, enabling his exclusive enforcement of these provisions. The fact that the state of exception arises from the "democratic-revolutionary tradition and not the absolutist one" is pertinent to the understanding of how the institution came to be emancipated from the circumstances of war that originally restricted its employment (Agamben 2005, 5). In the modern democratic state, the state of exception has morphed into "an extraordinary police measure to cope with internal sedition and disorder," and the category of war has moved from substantive to spurious, thus became markedly political (Agamben 2005, 5). The imposing of the state of exception is usually legitimised by the pronouncement of necessity. *Necessitas legem non habet* ("necessity has no law") can be simultaneously interpreted as "necessity does not recognise any law" and "necessity creates its own law" (Agamben 2005, 24). What follows is that the installation of necessity abandons the law, whose paramount objective is to ensure the welfare of the public, "in favour of expediency" (Agamben 2005, 46). Thus, the state of exception is not the space of absolute law, but "a space devoid of law" (Agamben 2005, 50).

The normalisation of the employment of the state of exception by modern Western states has led to the blurring of boundaries between executive and legislative powers. The latter has become increasingly cannibalised by the former, to the point where the legislative body no longer really produces the law, but simply ratifies the legal decisions of the executive order (Agamben 2005, 18). Furthermore, the state of exception, as situation which brings the law to a standstill, engenders the crisis of the legitimised violence. As Max Weber recognised in his essay "Politics as a Vocation," the definitive characteristic of the state is its monopoly on the legitimised use of violence, and this violence can be employed either in law-making or law-preserving capacity. However, the violence enacted by the state when functioning under the state of exception lacks relationality to the law due to its suspension, thus, producing what Walter Benjamin termed "pure violence" (qtd. in Agamben 2005, 53). Since the law cannot tolerate violence enacted outside of the scope of its territory, pure violence constitutes not only an act of unseating violence from the law, but the inauguration of an entirely new order. Pure violence, however, should not be misunderstood as the originary fodder of human activity that must be seized and shaped by the legal order, but rather "the stake in the conflict over the state of exception," and its occurrence marks the victory of exception over law (Agamben 2005, 60). What is particularly worrying about the state of exception, and by extension its widespread application in contemporary politics, is that it conjoins the spheres of the judicial and the political. These two spheres, although always correlated and in dialogue with each other, should be able to sustain the fiction of their separateness in order to maintain the functionality of the state. When that pretence collapses, "when the state of exception, in which they are bound and blurred together, becomes the rule, then the juridico-political system transforms itself into a killing machine" (Agamben 2005, 86). Though there is no returning to the state of law once a real state of exception has been established, due to the disintegration of the very concepts of "state" and "law," it is possible "to try to interrupt the working of the machine" by pronouncing the fiction at its centre and straining to keep the two forces trapped within it separate (Agamben 2005, 87). Considering the increasing weaponization of citizenship in contemporary British politics and the concerning scale of citizenship deprivation policies deemed by those in power as necessary measures, an argument can be made that Kamila Shamsie's *Home Fire* aims not only to represent the working of such a state, but to interrupt its fiction.

The return of banishment – suspect community, citizenship deprivation and its colonial hue

It is by no means an original statement to consider the situation of the "war on terror" as an example of the state of exception. What is of interest, however, to the consideration of *Home Fire* as a modern retelling of *Antigone* is the contemporary reinstatement of banishment (in the form of citizenship deprivation) motivated by the narrative propagated by the "war on terror" that the interests of national security warrant the employment of exceptional measures. Although, for the purposes of this chapter, I will focus on the increasing employment of citizenship deprivation powers by the British government, it is by no means an isolated precedent. Notably, the practice of citizenship stripping as a means of punishment has been on the increase in countries such as France, Canada, and Australia (Fargues 2017; Kingston 2021).

Within the context of British law, it is important to remember that citizenship is a relatively novel concept, one which replaced the notion of subjecthood upon the disintegration of the British Empire.

The British Nationality Act 1948 delineated that all royal subjects, thus both those residing on the British Isles and in the colonies, would hold British citizenship (Choudhury 2017; Naqvi 2022). Drawn up in response to the Canadian Citizenship Act to distinguish between British and Commonwealth citizens, who, previously, were all British subjects (Naqvi 2022), the BNA ensured "the right to enter, reside and work" in the United Kingdom of all British and Commonwealth citizens. The BNA also established a relatively straight-forward procedure of receiving British citizenship as it focused on the time spent in the UK by the applicant and avoided the implementation of such vague concepts as "British values" (Choudhury 2017, 230–231). In the decades following the initial BNA, the conception of citizenship, as well as Britishness, moved from relatively pragmatic to more overtly ideological. Markedly, the public discourse on who should be a British citizen was to come to obscure more tangible characteristics, such as birthplace or where a person spent the majority of their lives, in favour of "shared values," which upon further inspection betray themselves as refurbished imperialist narratives (Naqvi 2022; Webber 2022).

The issues of citizenship, the grounds upon which it is granted and the controversy surrounding its removal, arise from the fact that, as Hannah Arendt argued, citizenship constitutes "the right to have rights" (qtd. in Webber 2022, 78). The paramount importance of citizenship for the accessibility and feasibility of human rights is reflected in the international law prohibiting (albeit with some exceptions) the removal of citizenship if it would render an individual stateless (Choudhury 2017; Kingston 2021). It is important to note that the legal provisions that enable the executive powers to strip people of their British citizenship have always been inscribed within the British law, but by the middle of the 20th century, they largely fell into disuse. To put it into perspective, in the period between 1973 and 2002 there was no instance of citizenship deprivation in the UK. However, in 2017 alone, when the so-called caliphate of ISIL was collapsing and many British citizens who left the UK to join it were expressing their wish to repatriate, 104 people were stripped of their citizenship (Webber 2022, 80). Moreover, following the 7/7 terrorist attack, the British government quickly passed the Immigration, Asylum and Nationality Act 2005 which lowered the threshold for justified citizenship deprivation to one that would be "conducive to the public good" (Masters and Regilme 2020, 346), essentially deeming any arbitrary judgement of the executive branch as lawful grounds for such removals.

This policy of the British government of the last two decades to remove the citizenship of British nationals affiliated with terrorist organisations as a punitive measure is more detrimental to British society than it may at first appear. As international law largely blocks citizenship removal for people who hold only one citizenship, it creates a two-tiered system of citizenship. People with dual citizenship, such as children of immigrants who often have a right to the citizenship of the country of their parents' origin due to *jus sanguinis*, essentially find themselves having a conditional British citizenship (Fargues 2017). Particularly worrying in this regard is the recent case of Shamima Begum, who left the UK at the age of 15 to become a so-called 'ISIS bride' with two other girls, later dubbed the Bethnal Green three. In 2019, she requested to be allowed to come back to the UK to give birth to her third child, after her previous two died in infancy. The Home Secretary at the time, Sajid Javid, whose rise to the office was eerily and unintentionally foreseen by Kamila Shamsie in *Home Fire* (Shamsie 2018b), decided on the revocation of Begum's citizenship, despite her holding only British citizenship. He claimed that since Begum could technically apply for Bangladeshi citizenship due to her mother being from there, the decision would not really render her stateless (Masters and Regilme 2020).

Unsurprisingly, the Bangladeshi government disavowed Begum and she is, at the time of writing this chapter, still stateless. What Shamima Begum's case also represents is the tendency of the British government "towards a policy of exporting its way out of the threat from home grown terrorism" (Choudhury 2017, 235) and treating "the rest of the world [as their] penal colony (...) where they can abandon undesirable citizens through modern-day exile" (Naqvi 2022, 525). Rather than recognising its own liability, the government washes its hands clean of individuals who became radicalised while still in the UK, essentially asserting that citizenship is a privilege, not a right, ignoring the fact that a government is to be responsible for all its citizens, even those who commit the most heinous of crimes.

There is another worrying precedent set forth by using citizenship deprivation as a punitive measure in cases of British nationals that joined terrorist groups such as ISIL. Due to the limited ability to garner accounts of the conduct and evidence of crimes possibly committed while part of the organisation, it is then a punishment meted out on the presumption of criminality. It is a shift from a "post-crime" to a "pre-crime" society, in which punishment can be inflicted for a crime that is hypothetical (Choudhury 2017, 236–237). This, in turn, facilitates a paranoia of suspicion regarding the British Muslim community, precipitated by the narrative of terrorism occurring due to the values of the radicalised individuals being divergent from "British values." This foregrounds the perception that the home-grown terrorism is a "failure of integration caused by too much multiculturalism" (Choudhury 2017, 238). Which is to say that the British Muslim community is, and has been since 9/11, the new suspect community in the UK. Similarly to the Irish community in respect to which the term was first coined by Paddy Hiliyard, members of the British Muslim community are thrust into the criminal justice system on the basis of their identity alone – their actual behaviour is secondary for the presumption of wrongdoing (Lynch 2013; Frank 2021). This assumption that radicalisation and the acts of terrorism that it spurs have their root in the Muslim identity, both as a religious and a socio-political identity, leads to the misunderstanding of what predominantly entices young people to terrorist ideologies and what Islam constitutes to the majority of British Muslims.

The misguided belief that Islam plays a pivotal role in the radicalisation of British Muslim youth propels the narrative that Muslim and British identities are mutually exclusionary (Lynch 2013). One of the reasons for the distrust regarding the loyalties of the British Muslim community and the incessant broadcasting of the perceived necessity to integrate them is the secularisation and general fall in religiosity of British society throughout the 20th century, which establishes the still relatively religious Muslim minority as the cultural Other (Sobolewska 2010; Naqvi 2022). However, the establishment of a distinctively British Islam, which, as Orla Lynch has argued, is "a scriptural (rather than cultural) interpretation," allows British Muslim youth to establish their understanding of Islam within the British cultural context (Lynch 2013, 252). This reframing of cultural terms in respect of the religion they follow, in lieu of adhering to the cultural interpretation of their parents' or grandparents' generation that has migrated to the UK, is precisely a proof of assimilation, not isolation (Lynch 2013). Which is not to say that Islam or ideas expressed within its doctrine are not weaponised for the purposes of radicalisation and subsequent recruitment, but it is important to recognise the order of causality. Islam can be instrumental to the process of radicalisation but is not endemic to it (Githens-Mazer 2010). This becomes all the more evident when we consider radicalisation as a social process, rather than an ideological one.

Radicalisation as a crisis of the self and mourning as a crisis of the state in *Home Fire*

The clinging by both the general public and governmental policy in the UK to the unsubstantiated claim in respect to Islam and the radicalisation its observance supposedly leads to is partially motivated by the elusive nature of the process of radicalisation itself. The primary factors of radicalisation are social, not ideological. It is strong social dynamics, especially those through which an individual can experience for the first time a strong sense of praise, respect, and validation, that make one susceptible to more radical ideas and, subsequently, radical acts (Githens-Mazer 2010; Chambers 2018). What is problematic about this pattern is that it is more akin to the healthy identity formation of young people through socialisation than it is dissimilar, thus it is difficult to police and spot in the early stages of the process. In *Home Fire*, as Chambers argues, Parvaiz is made vulnerable by "the crisis of masculinity" he is experiencing, similarly to many other 19-year-olds (Chambers 2018, 206). It is this vulnerability that makes him so susceptible to his recruiter's charm and the extremist ideas he so charismatically bestows on the young man. When asked why she had not informed authorities sooner about her brother's radicalisation that led to his departure for ISIL, Isma retorts that she simply thought that it was "his first time in love [and that] in a way, it was" (Shamsie 2018a, 238).

In an interview with *The Jakarta Post*, Kamila Shamsie admitted that what drew her to Sophocles' *Antigone* was the fundamentally antithetical reactions of two sisters to their brother's treason (Heriyanto 2018). Though the traditional opposition of Antigone and Creon is also recreated in Shamsie's modern retelling of the play through the characters of Aneeka and Karamat and their ideological clash, with its fatal consequences, *Home Fire* foregrounds and explores the sororal conflict in detail. The novel emphasises that the most intimate and devastating tragedy in both texts derives not from the contention against the state and its law, but from the insoluble dissension between the love owed to the living and the love owed to the dead. Unconstrained by the rules of the Greek theatre, though still referencing and subverting its traditional structure (cf. Weiss 2022), Shamsie's narrative in *Home Fire* expands beyond the single act of rebellion, painting in great detail what kind of experience of reality presupposes such a radical disobedience. The novel, split into five parts, each from a different character's perspective, dives deeper into the characters and their psychology beyond their representative moral choices within the story. It problematises further the question to whom (or to what) one should remain faithful that was first explored in *Antigone*.

Similarly to the Sophoclean play, in *Home Fire* there is a young man that betrayed his country (here, by joining ISIL) and is refused burial in his home nation on the grounds of his treason. His two sisters, his sibling-parent Isma and fraternal twin Aneeka, clash on what is the right thing to do. Isma believes that out of fidelity to each other, as the only family either of them have left, they ought to stay safe, obey the law even if it is unjust and mourn their brother privately. Aneeka, who before her brother's death tried to arrange his safe return to London from Syria, believes that the only moral thing they could do, if they failed to bring their brother home, was to bring his body home. Hellbent on honouring her brother, Aneeka strives against Karamat Lone, a Conservative Home Secretary, who stripped her brother, Parvaiz, of citizenship in retribution for his treason. Karamat's son and Aneeka's lover, Eamonn, tries to convince his father to relent and see the error of his headstrong, unforgiving policy, but to no avail. Just as in the play, the novel ends with the deaths of Aneeka and Eamonn, who are blown up after Eamonn has a suicide vest put on him – a moment captured on camera and replayed endlessly on news channels for Karamat and his wife to watch. The scene serves as a sombre reminder of Karamat's own criticism levied against his firstborn son when Eamonn decided to publicly support his fiancée in her protest against the British government and join her in Pakistan. When asked by a member of his staff why he did not ask the Pakistani officials to intervene and put Eamonn on a flight back to England, Karamat says of his son: "(...) he's a British national who made a choice and has to face the consequences. As any other British national would" (Shamsie 2018a, 238). The quote also illustrates a layer of the story unexplored in the original play, but instrumental both to the mechanisms of the novel's plot and to the moral implications of the characters' decisions. Namely, the issue of citizenship, or more specifically, the issue of Britishness, and how its weaponization as a privilege in the supposedly postcolonial Britain is the true tragedy-engineering hubris.

In chapters describing the recruitment and radicalisation of Parvaiz, we see Farooq, Parvaiz's recruiter, exploit his sense of disenfranchisement in the austerity state and desire for not only a just law, but a law that ensures justice. As such it emerges, as Debjani Banerjee argued, that the novel is conscious of the fact that radicalisation "can be understood as part of a historical encounter" (Banerjee 2020, 296). Considering that all the main characters are Brits of Pakistani descent, the problematisation of whose law and whose justice within the postcolonial context clearly materializes. When Aneeka announces to TV reporters that she is going to Pakistan (where her brother's body was sent for burial) for justice, Karamat's immediate reaction is that of contempt – not just for her act of disobedience, but for the mere suggestion that Pakistan is where the law and justice reside. Watching her on TV, he says:

"She's going to look for justice in *Pakistan*?" That final word spoken with all the disgust of a child of migrants who understands how much his parents gave up – family, context, language, familiarity – because the nation to which they first belonged had proven itself inadequate to the task of allowing them to live with dignity. (Shamsie 2018a, 215)

It is hard to ignore the eurocentrism at the core of Karamat's hypocrisy. For him, the idea of justice in a state such as Pakistan is contemptible, for the law there, as the apparatus of justice, does not serve its people, thus is not just. And for the law to remain just in the United Kingdom it must remain unfazed in the face of people that demand it should serve them better, more justly. Thus, Karamat's position is an echo chamber of the voices in British politics and society that call for "the imposition of a homogenous British identity" so that the law could serve all of them justly (Banerjee 2020, 292). However, it would be myopic to interpret that Karamat's adherence to the law stems from his self-interest. Rather, like Parvaiz, he let himself become consumed and corrupted by an idea he loved too desperately to love it critically.

Treason, (dis)obedience and the condition of the law in *Antigone* and *Home Fire*

One of the most interesting changes in *Home Fire* in regard to the original characterisation in *Antigone* is the character of Isma. In the play, Ismene's choice of pragmatism is largely overshadowed by the antipodal ideologies of Antigone and Creon, though in this clash of the self-righteous, Ismene seems the only morally sober character. During the opening scene, when Antigone first discloses her plan to her sister, hoping she would join her, Ismene refuses, chastising her for being foolish and accusing her of wilful ignorance of the political reality of the situation and their position as women in the society.

In this regard, I would like to briefly entertain an unorthodox reading of the play, which suggests that it is Ismene who was responsible for the first burial (Honig 2011; Kirkpatrick 2011). This interpretation is largely motivated by the fact that there is little in the text to support why Antigone would bury Polynices twice, and why a character as rigid and absolutist in her assertions as to what is right and proper would do such a provisional job with the first burial. Moreover, it introduces a more interesting presentation of Ismene as a foil of Antigone. It becomes not so much a case of Ismene being too weak to act, but rather acting from the position of the weak. Therefore, Antigone and Ismene are not a coupling of action and inaction, but rather of the heroic and the unheroic. Furthermore, the seemingly insoluble conflict of Antigone and Creon is soluble through the unheroic approach, i.e. to bury Polynices provisionally in secret, so the necessary burial rites are administered, albeit poorly, and feign obedience to the edict and the state in public. Though the argument could be made that such an approach reinstates the status quo, it would also prevent the onslaught of violence characterising the conclusion of the play.[2]

Home Fire not only reiterates this sobriety of consideration in the stance Isma takes in the central conflict of the novel but also fleshes out Isma to be a representative of a perspective even more nuanced. In

---

[2] Jennet Kirkpatrick also points out that "according to Athenian custom, two actions were required for the successful transition of the soul to the netherworld: the administration of burial rites and the fulfilment of the *eniausia*, the annual commemorative visits to the tomb (...) the requirements of *eniuasia* are especially noteworthy because they demand something that, if both sisters act recklessly, Polyneices may lack: a living relative" (2011, 49).

the novel, Isma is accused of betraying Aneeka not once, but twice – when she reports to the Metropolitan Police that Parvaiz has joined ISIL and when she refuses to join Aneeka in her public demand to return his body to the UK. Not unlike Ismene, Isma wants to keep her and Aneeka safe, but where the novel goes beyond the original play is in its portrayal of just how frail the laboriously achieved safety of a suspect community is. The opening scene of the novel itself is that of an airport interrogation that Isma is forced to endure for hours just to be allowed to board her flight to Amherst, Massachusetts, where she was to begin her PhD studies in sociology. Isma, unlike Aneeka, whose youth grants her rigid idealism, is acutely aware that they are always one misstep away from suspicions of fanaticism. She is aware that for British Muslims, especially those of working-class background, the experience of being suspected is almost indistinguishable from the experience of being sentenced. Moreover, Isma's perspective is further complicated by the hybrid role she is forced to enact in her siblings' life. After the death of their mother and grandmother, Isma, then not yet 21, becomes the parental figure to her 12-year-old siblings. Neither a mother nor a sister, but a mother-sister, Isma[3] does not have the liberty to mourn the loss of Parvaiz, first to radicalism, then to death, when her sister-child is in real need of protection – the complex circumstances wrongly rebuffed as lack of loyalty and love by Aneeka. I would even go as far as to argue that if there is a model of behaviour that we should encourage both individuals and the state to follow, it is that of Isma: one that puts care over righteousness.

---

[3]   What makes this subversion even more interesting is the fact that, although Ismene is traditionally interpreted to be older than Antigone, within the Sophoclean text itself there is no designation of the age difference of the sisters, for, unlike in the case of fraternity, primogeniture historically had no impact on the sororal relationships (cf. Goldhill 2006).

The two overarching themes for both texts are the relationship between the law and justice and the issue of the state: should its people be faithful to it, or should it be faithful to its people? First, let's consider the problem of the law. As Creon's sovereignty merges in itself both judicial and executive powers, he both makes the law and executes it, to similarly lethal effects like the state of exception discussed earlier. This conception of lawfulness as stemming from a single person yet enforced on everybody is further criticised within the play during the confrontation between Haemon and Creon:

CREON
Who's to take charge? The ruler or the ruled?
HAEMON
There's no city that belongs in single hands,
CREON
Rulers, I thought, were meant to be in charge.
HAEMON
Where you should be in charge is in a desert. (Heaney 2004, 33)

The law is seen as the preeminent value – the ultimate virtue that must be protected from the people that wish to tarnish it, rather than the apparatus of extending protection over the people. Creon, as the king, is not only the primary agent of the law, but its embodiment and this is the condition of his tragedy. By embracing his identity as the law, he hollowed out his own humanity and it is as this shell of a person filled to the brim with the power of the law that he enacts cruelty – on others, but vitally also on himself. Such is also the condition of Karamat's tragedy. In a brief scene towards the end of the book, Shamsie clearly envisions Karamat as a pious adherer of the law, who empties himself to absorb the law with the same zeal a religious man prostrates himself before God and His wisdom:

> [The] man had slicked-back hair and black mark on his forehead – the latter a sign of piety, helped along by deliberately banging one's head against a stone or rough surface during all the daily prostrating in prayer. Karamat picked up a lion-and-unicorn paperweight, pressed it to this forehead. (Shamsie 2018a, 220)

It is important to note that all the characters in the novel subscribe to the notion that good law presupposes the existence of a good society, with the notable difference being that Karamat, unlike Isma, Aneeka, and later Eamonn, believes the law to already be good and it is its reluctant appliance and enforcement that impedes social welfare.

Both *Home Fire* and *Antigone* investigate the fraudulent assertion of treason as a unidirectional crime – that only a citizen can betray their country. As clearly evident in *Home Fire*, it is the state's betrayal of the citizen that more often than not precedes the citizen's betrayal of the state. Yet, the state, more so than the law, is deemed infallible. The state's politicians, the state's systems, even the state's law may fail people, but never the state itself. And it is this perceived utmost fidelity of the state that in turn makes treason such an abominable crime and allows the endorsement of policies that treat citizenship as a privilege rather than a human right. However, both texts recognise that the reality of this perception is entirely contingent on which state you get to experience – that of the carer or that of the enforcer. This clash of experiences is quickly made evident in *Home Fire*, when Isma explains to Eamonn what happened to her and her family when her father left to become a mujahideen:

"A few months later MI5 and Special Branch Officers came around asking for him, though they wouldn't say why. We knew something was wrong, and my grandmother said maybe we should try to contact someone – the Red Cross, the government, a lawyer – to find out where he was. My grandmother went to the mosque to look for support, but the Imam sided with my mother – he'd heard too many stories of abuse suffered by the families of British men who'd been arrested in Afghanistan. One of my grandmother's friends had said that the British government would withdraw all the benefits of the welfare state – including state school and the NHS – from any family it suspected of siding with the terrorists." Eamonn made a face of distaste, clearly offended in a way that told her he saw the state as part of himself, something that had never been possible for anyone in her family. (Shamsie 2018a, 49)

Both *Home Fire* and *Antigone* examine what becomes of the state that refuses to be faithful to its citizens; how fast and freely violence spreads when the state deems itself entitled to instigate it; how uncritical fidelity leads to cruelty. It is interesting to consider that, strictly speaking, Parvaiz did not break any laws. He never killed anyone while part of ISIL, never recruited nor shared information detrimental to the safety of the state. Though an argument can easily be made that enhancing the audio in the video recordings of executions and not helping an uncovered woman while she lies crushed by a fallen building are ethically reprehensible, they are not criminal. It is only turning his back on his country that he is guilty of – a country that has turned its back on him and his family, yet only one of these treasons warrants punishment. And although Parvaiz is an entirely fictional character, the conduct by the British government and judiciary depicted in the novel is anything but fictitious.

Conclusion

In *Sweet Violence*, Terry Eagleton professes that for a tragedy to be tragic it can neither be fully of fate nor fully of will, but instead must emerge from the ambiguous element of the human condition where the line between agency and predetermination is blurred. A space where "purposive action always has its residue of the non-intended [and], as the notion of peripeteia would suggest, [where] non-intentional actions are also the by-product of purposes" (Eagleton 2009, 125). What else is this space but history? What else is history but pertinacious currents of events that are neither accidental nor intentional, but somehow always inexplicitly both? Can we ever, as Parvaiz wished, "break out of these currents of history, (...) shake free of the demons (...) attached to [our] own heels" (Shamsie 2018a, 171)? It is the vagaries of history that decide what state we belong to and in what form we encounter it – whether we are able to enjoy the privilege of its protection or bear the brunt of its interests. We cannot escape and we do not seem to be able to learn from it, but we can at least become more sympathetic to the enormous weight of its burden.

References

Agamben, Giorgio. 1998. *Homo Sacer. Sovereign Power and Bare Life*. Translated by Daniel Heller-Roazen. Stanford, CA. Stanford University Press.

—. 2005. *State of Exception*. Translated by Kevin Attell. Chicago and London. The University of Chicago Press.

Banerjee, Debjani. 2020. "From Cheap Labor to Overlooked Citizens: Looking for British Muslim Identities in Kamila Shamsie's Home Fire." *South Asian Review* 41(3–4), 288–302. https://doi.org/10.1080/02759527.2020.1835141

Butler, Judith. 2000. *Antigone's Claim: Kinship Between Life & Death*. New York. Columbia University Press.

Chambers, Claire. 2018. "Sound and Fury: Kamila Shamsie's Home Fire." *The Massachusetts Review* 59(2), 202–219. https://doi.org/10.1353/mar.2018.0029

Choudhury, Tufyal. 2017. "The Radicalisation of Citizenship Deprivation." *Critical Social Policy* 37(2), 225–244. https://doi.org/10.1177/0261018316684507

Eagleton, Terry. 2009. *Sweet Violence: The Idea of the Tragic*. New York, NY. John Wiley & Sons.

Fargues, Émilien. 2017. "The Revival of Citizenship Deprivation in France and the UK as an Instance of Citizenship Renationalisation." *Citizenship Studies* 21(8), 984–998. https://doi.org/10.1080/13621025.2017.1377152

Frank, Michael C. 2021. "'The Insecurity State': Anti-Terrorism Legislation and the Politics of Fear in Kamila Shamsie's 'Home Fire.'" *Journal for the Study of British Cultures* 28(2), 209–223.

Githens-Mazer, Jonathan. 2010. "Mobilization, Recruitment, Violence and the Street. Radical Violent *Takfiri* Islamism in Early Twenty-First-Century Britain." In: *The New Extremism in 21st Century Britain*. Eds. Roger Eatwell and Matthew J. Goodwin. New York. Routledge, 47–66.

Goldhill, Simon. 2006. "Antigone and the Politics of Sisterhood." In: *Laughing with Medusa. Classical Myth and Feminist Thought*. Eds. Vanda Zajko and Miriam Leonard. Oxford. Oxford University Press, 141–162.

Heaney, Seamus. 2004. *The Burial at Thebes. Sophocles' Antigone*. London. Faber & Faber.

Heriyanto, Devina. 2018. "Interview: Kamila Shamsie Talks About 'Home Fire', Minorities and Terrorism." https://www.thejakartapost.com/life/2018/04/04/interview-kamila-shamsie-talks-about-home-fire-minorities-and-terrorism.html (accessed 10 February 2023).

Honig, Bonnie. 2009. "Antigone's Laments, Creon's Grief: Mourning, Membership, and the Politics of Exception." *Political Theory* 37(1), 5–43. www.jstor.org/stable/20452679

—. 2010. "Antigone's Two Laws: Greek Tragedy and the Politics of Humanism." *New Literary History* 41(1), 1–33. www.jstor.org/stable/40666482

—. 2011. "Ismene's Forced Choice: Sacrifice and Sorority in Sophocles' *Antigone*." *Arethusa* 44(1), 29–68. https://doi.org/10.1353/are.2011.a413524

Kingston, Lindsey N. 2021. "The Weaponisation of Citizenship: Punishment, Erasure, and Social Control." In: *Statelessness, Governance, and the Problem of Citizenship*. Eds. Tendayi Bloom and Lindsey N. Kingston. Manchester and New York. Manchester University Press, 99–111.

Kirkpatrick, Jennet. 2011. "The Prudent Dissident: Unheroic Resistance in Sophocles' Antigone." *The Review of Politics* 73(3), 401–424. https://www.jstor.org/stable/23016517

Krause, Peter. 2020. "*Antigone* in Pakistan: *Home Fire*, by Kamila Shamsie." *Journal of Comparative Literature* 43(3). Supplement, 13–22.

Lauriola, Rosanna. 2007. "Wisdom and Foolishness: A Further Point in the Interpretation of Sophocles' Antigone." *Hermes* 135(4), 389–405. www.jstor.org/stable/40379138

Leonard, Miriam. 2006. "Lacan, Irigaray, and Beyond: Antigones and the Politics of Psychoanalysis." In: *Laughing with Medusa. Classical Myth and Feminist Thought*. Eds. Vanda Zajko and Miriam Leonard. Oxford. Oxford University Press, 121–140.

Lynch, Orla. 2013. "British Muslim Youth: Radicalisation, Terrorism and the Construction of the 'Other'." *Critical Studies on Terrorism* 6(2), 241–261. https://doi.org/10.1080/17539153.2013.788863

Masters, Mercedes and Salvador Santino Regilme. 2020. "Human Rights and British Citizenship: The Case of Shamima Begum as Citizen to Homo Sacer." *Journal of Human Rights Practice* 12(2), 341–363. https://doi.org/10.1093/jhuman/huaa029

Meltzer, Françoise. 2011. "Theories of Desire: Antigone Again." *Critical Inquiry* 37(2), 169–186. https://doi.org/10.1086/657289

Naqvi, Zainab Batu. 2022. "Coloniality, Belonging and Citizenship Deprivation in the UK: Exploring Judicial Responses." *Social & Legal Studies* 31(4), 516–534.

Robert, William. 2010. "Antigone's Nature." *Hypatia* 25(2), 412–436.

Shamsie, Kamila. 2018a. *Home Fire*. London. Bloomsbury Publishing.
—. 2018b. "True Story: Kamila Shamsie on Predicting the Rise of Sajid Javid." https://www.theguardian.com/books/booksblog/2018/may/03/true-story-kamila-shamsie-on-predicting-the-rise-of-sajid-javid (accessed 20 July 2023).
—. 2022. "A Hostile Environment Baton Passed from Theresa May to Priti Patel – and a Decade of Cruelty." www.theguardian.com/commentisfree/2022/jun/23/hostile-environment-theresa-may-priti-patel-rwanda-deportation (accessed 20 July 2023).
Sobolewska, Maria. 2010. "Religious Extremism in Britain and British Muslims. Threatened Citizenship and the Role of Religion." In: *The New Extremism in 21st Century Britain*. Eds. Roger Eatwell and Matthew J. Goodwin. New York. Routledge, 23–46.
Webber, Frances. 2022. "The Racialisation of British Citizenship." *Race & Class* 64(2), 75–93. https://doi.org/10.1177/03063968221117950
Weiss, Naomi. 2022. "Tragic Form in Kamila Shamsie's Home Fire." *Classical Receptions Journal* 14(2), 240–263. https://doi.org/10.1093/crj/clab008
Wiltshire, Susan Ford. 1976. "Antigone's Disobedience." *Arethusa* 9(1), 29–36.

WIKTORIA WAWRZYŃCZYK

2.
Stitches and Stories: Ahmed Saadawi's *Frankenstein in Baghdad*

Introduction

Daniel Cottom once wrote of Frankenstein's creature that he is "a likeness of the novel itself" (1980, 60). Although he professed this in connection to the concept of "the monstrous nature of representation," suggesting that Shelley's novel may induce a similar feeling of terror in the reader as the monster induced in Victor Frankenstein (1980, 60), such a comment may be applied more literally, pointing to the structural resemblance between the character and the book. Lisa Vargo, for example, emphasises their metatextual kinship when she argues that "like the creature, who is the product of gathered materials, the novel itself is a palimpsest of Mary Shelley's own reading" (2016, 26). It is composed, constructed, of different parts, both in terms of the iconic frame narrative and multiple literary and cultural contexts which contributed to its final shape.

A similar relationship emerges even more vividly in a modern variation of *Frankenstein* written by an Iraqi author, Ahmed Saadawi, and titled *Frankenstein in Baghdad*. The novel, which was awarded the International Prize for Arabic Fiction in 2014, features a figure of "the Whatsitsname" ("Shesma" in the Arabic original), whose body is carefully but not quite seamlessly stitched from numerous smaller pieces. The closer one examines how the entire book is structured, in terms of the thematic, narrative and compositional dimensions, the clearer it becomes that this motif of fragmentation and incongruity serves as a dominant concept permeating almost every layer of the text. In this chapter, I will discuss this complex relationship between the form and the content of Saadawi's novel, pointing out what effect it achieves on each layer, how it reveals the author's metatextual awareness, and how it helps him to engage with the ailments and crises of contemporary reality. In the first part of the text, I will focus on the problems of violence, justice and criminality, as well as the terrifying conditions of living in post-2003 Iraq, mostly drawing on the observations of other researchers who emphasised the sociopolitical context of the book. The second part will be devoted to a detailed analysis of the novel's structure, paratextual and metatextual elements, framing devices, complexity of the plot and narration. Finally, I will move on to discuss the nuances of storytelling, unreliability, persuasion and manipulation, the power of words and the relativity of truth.[1]

---

[1] This text is heavily based on my BA thesis, titled *Ahmed Saadawi's "Frankenstein in Baghdad"* – its structure, narration and engagement with Mary Shelley's *Frankenstein*, submitted and defended at the Jagiellonian University, Institute of English Studies

It is not easy to summarise *Frankenstein in Baghdad* in a clear and coherent way, due to the multiplicity of subplots, which cross and intertwine, following a large number of different characters. Even so, I will attempt to provide a general outline to serve as a reference point for the reader who is not familiar with Saadawi's novel. The events take place in Baghdad, in the district of Bataween to be exact. Iraq is under the American occupation. Violence and terror are a part of daily life, to the point of being treated with casual matter-of-factness.[2] Hadi, a local junk-dealer known for his storytelling skills, undertakes a peculiar mission: he gathers fragments of corpses he finds on the streets and stitches them together, to create a complete body and hand it over to the authorities "so it would be respected like other dead people and given a proper burial" (Saadawi 2018, 27). Eventually, "the Whatsitsname" is finished, but before Hadi has a chance to finalise his plan, the body gets inhabited by a wandering soul of a hotel guard killed in a terrorist attack earlier the same day. It is then awakened by an old Christian woman living next door. This elderly lady is Elishva, whose son, Daniel, was lost in the Iraq-Iran war of 1980–1988 and is presumed dead. Determined to believe that her son is alive, she mistakes the mysterious figure she sees for him and names him "Daniel," thus giving him a symbolic identity.

---

in 2022. The chapter contains extensive quotations from the thesis, which will not be separately referenced.

[2] At one point the reader learns that "[Hadi] went to see Edward Boulos, the man who sold alcohol. Edward has closed his little shop overlooking the Umma Garden because someone had thrown a hand grenade at it early one morning, setting fire to it. After that he moved his business, the only one he knew, into his house" (Saadawi 2018, 88). Violence is treated as something that does not deserve attention in itself, but only in connection to other matters.

The creature gains awareness and embarks on a mission – he has to avenge all the victims his body is composed of. Whenever he kills a person responsible for the death of one of them, the corresponding piece of his body rots and falls away. Therefore, in order to remain functional, the Whatsitsname needs a constant supply of the flesh of victims to replace the missing parts. His activity leads to various more and less mysterious and violent occurrences in a place already chaotic and mad, even without a living corpse haunting its streets. Among those who want to learn more about the mysterious criminal are the local authorities, the Tracking and Pursuit Department led by Brigadier Majid, and journalists, particularly Mahmoud al-Sawadi, who is another major figure in the story. Due to a conflict with a gang leader in his hometown, Mahmoud was forced to move to Baghdad, where he faces new challenges, gains experience and gradually matures. Having heard the full story of the Whatsitsname from Hadi, he quickly becomes interested and indirectly interviews the mysterious avenger via a recorder Hadi passes between them. This recording is the central part of the novel, which corresponds with the creature's tale in *Frankenstein*. The Whatsitsname explains the motives behind his actions, describes how a group of "assistants" gathered around him, attracting more and more followers until they formed a complex, hierarchical structure, and how this structure eventually fell apart because of internal conflicts which ended in a massacre. In contrast to the creature's tale in Shelley's novel, the recording is rather impersonal in tone and resembles a manifesto more than a confession. It seems to be in keeping with how the Whatsitsname is portrayed throughout the novel. He often appears to serve more as a concept, a trigger for the events than a character with a complex personality. Therefore, despite his account being the core of the book's physical structure, other perspectives, particularly Mahmoud's, Hadi's and Elishva's, are featured much more frequently.

The fragmented body and the world shattered by war

The majority of researchers who have close-read *Frankenstein in Baghdad* have paid much attention to the sociopolitical layer of Saadawi's novel, quite understandably, since the entire story depends on the wartime setting, the horrors and the paradoxes of Iraq reality. It is also in this context that they most often mention the motif of fragmentation and incongruity. Alhashmi stresses the dystopian and grotesque qualities of *Frankenstein in Baghdad*, noting how Saadawi mixes elements of realism, exaggeration and fantasy to foreground the surreal and horrifying conditions of living in Iraq (2020, 92). Murphy describes the social and political reality of Baghdad as characterised by instability and precariousness, discussing "precarization" as a mode of governance (2018, 280). To him, the Whatsitsname's body is a metaphor of violence and "the instrumentalization of human bodies in conditions of contemporary violent conflict" (Murphy 2018, 278). Bahoora also sees his body in a symbolic manner, as "a metaphor for the fragmented and injured nation (...) representing various incarnations of Iraqi identity" (2015, 196). This is an important remark, especially in the context of how the Bataween area is described in the novel. It is said to have "plenty of outsiders who had moved in on top of each other over many decades; no one could claim to be an original inhabitant" (Saadawi 2018, 23). The inhabitants differ in terms of their background, ancestry and religion. The idea that the Whatsitsname may be seen as a representative, a kind of icon for all these diversities is introduced directly by the "young madman," one of his followers, who sees the mysterious avenger as the "first true Iraqi citizen" (Saadawi 2018, 147), as he is "made up of body parts of people from diverse backgrounds – ethnicities, tribes, races and social classes" (146). He may therefore be read as a cultural hybrid, a person of fluid identity, constantly in the process of creation. Bahoora notes, however, that a more pessimistic reading is also possible, suggesting that "the supernaturally created corpse is the ideal to which the reality of Iraq has failed to live up" (2015, 196).

On the one hand, therefore, the Whatsitsname stands for the ordinary people of Baghdad, the oppressed, the victims; both in the symbolic and literal sense – after all, that is his purpose, to avenge the innocent. Nonetheless, his strategy and the mechanism of sustaining his life pose many ethical questions: How far can one go in punishing criminals before becoming a criminal oneself? How to judge who is guilty and who is innocent? Saadawi dissects the never-ending cycle of cruelty and the ambiguity of the avenger's position – if someone kills a person in an act of revenge, it does not make them any less of a killer themselves. So, ultimately, justice is impossible to reach, because vengeance inevitably creates new criminals. Besides, often there is not a single person to blame, but many people share the responsibility, making society a complicated mixture of innocence and guilt which cannot be separated from each other – "each of us has a measure of criminality" (Saadawi 2018, 156). The matter is further complicated by the plurality of relative views on the question of which agenda may be considered righteous and thus legitimise extreme measures. Abdalkafor, who compares *Frankenstein* and *Frankenstein in Baghdad* through the lens of Agamben's *homo sacer* theory, stresses the aspect of complicated and chaotic power dynamics in the latter text. She points out that "In this novel, sovereignty is more complicated than expected as there are different parties claiming to be sovereign" (Abdalkafor 2018, 11). And later: "The novel is full of violence; every party thinks they are fighting for a valid reason and see their violence as lawful while others see it as lawless. All view [the Whatsitsnames's] violence as lawless though he himself considers he is achieving justice until his body becomes a mixture of criminals' as well as victims' flesh, contaminating his mission" (Abdalkafor 2018, 13). Eventually, his moral judgement becomes clouded and he is ready to deliberately kill a civilian in order to save his decomposing body (Saadawi 2018, 161) – a choice which he attempts to justify or at least rationalise, but which could have been dictated by simple survival instincts, working irrespectively of any noble ideas.

What emerges from this discussion is that the Whatsitsname serves both as a symbol of and as a protest against the terror and violence pervading the streets of Baghdad. It is not only his body that is constructed of incongruous pieces. His identity also resembles a patchwork more than a coherent whole. He is created by Hadi and awakened by Elishva, neither of whom is fully aware of what they are doing. They have one thing in common, however: their actions stem from tragedies and losses they have experienced. The origin of Hadi's project is traced back to the death of his close friend, Nahem Abdaki, which left him deeply traumatised (Saadawi 2018, 25). Elishva mistakes the body for her lost son, Daniel. Additionally, the soul which animates the Whatsitsname belongs to Hasib Mohamed Jaafar, the hotel guard killed in a terrorist attack while on duty. Therefore, all three of them – Nahem, Daniel and Hasib – serve as surrogate identities for the Whatsitsname in one way or another. Moreover, in all those cases of death there was no body left behind which could be given a proper burial. All that was left to represent them were clothes, pieces of a smashed guitar (in Daniel's case) or small body parts (in

Hasib's), again echoing the "fragmentation quality" so crucial to the novel.

Even his name, or rather names, reflect this. Elishva calls him "Daniel," astrologers working for Majid refer to him as "The One Who Has No Name," while the journalists dub him "Criminal X." "The Whatsitsname" is what Hadi calls him when he is retelling the story of his creation to other people. His identity is fluent and evolves together with his face, as it morphs into new forms after bits and pieces fall away and are continuously replaced. But what makes the claim that he is "the likeness of the novel itself" so accurate? How does this motif of fragmentation and incongruity manifest itself on other layers of the book? This will be the main focus in the following section.

Fragmentation as a mode of organising and narrating the story

Admittedly, some scholars do note that the image of a fragmented body is echoed in the shape and form of the novel. Murphy observes that the narration oscillating between third-person and first-person mode, as well as the digressive way in which the story is developed and the large number of characters contribute to "a structure that expresses the very real situation of escalating violence and civilian casualties in Iraq during the US invasion, and the civil war which ensued" (2018, 280). Booker and Daraiseh make this even clearer, stating that "the novel's narrative, which contains a number of different components with different narrators and presumably different sources, is in fact stitched together very much in the same manner as the Whatsitsname" (2021). I wish to examine this interrelation in more detail, pointing out various ambiguities and dissonances and discussing the effect they have on the text and the reader.

Frankenstein in Baghdad includes many different textual and metatextual frames, which contribute to the collage feel of the entire novel. It begins with three epigraphs: a quote from *Frankenstein*, a passage from the story of St. George, and a fragment of the Whatsitsname's recording. Each of them has its own significance. The passage from Shelley's novel is very short: "Yet I ask you not to spare me: listen to me; and then, if you can, and if you will, destroy the work of your hands." It is an appeal to Victor Frankenstein's sense of justice, but also a testimony of the belief in the power of words, the impact of the story, an issue that I will elaborate on later in this chapter. In the context of Saadawi's text, it corresponds, of course, to the Whatsitsname's aim in revealing the details of his strategy to the public. He wants the truth – or what he considers to be the truth – to be known so that his mission is no longer confused with the actions of ordinary criminals (Saadawi 2018, 143).

The legend of St. George foreshadows the story of Hadi and the Whatsitsname, since the martyr was "placed in the olive press until his flesh was torn to pieces" but the pieces were later gathered by Jesus and St. George was revived. Moreover, as Booker and Daraiseh argue, "the inclusion of Saint George within the text makes clear that there are a number of stories from a variety of cultural traditions around the world that contain elements similar to those that drive this narrative," emphasising the complexity of the cultural network of associations which Saadawi's novel employs (2021). St. George is also a patron saint figure for Elishva, who has a large painting of him in her house and treats him "as one of her relatives" (Saadawi 2018, 15). She frequently talks to him, sometimes sharing her worries and sometimes scolding the saint for his lack of success in bringing her lost son back to her. At first glance this seems to signal Elishva's peculiar (not to say unsound) state of mind, but later, as various supernatural occurrences unfold, this painted figure is shown speaking to the Whatsitsname (Saadawi 2018, 56), prompting the reader to question not just Elishva's reliability, but all of their basic assumptions concerning the "realness" of the story. And closer to the end of the book, when Elishva is preparing to leave Baghdad, she cuts the head of St. George from the painting so that she can take it with her, which is yet another, although minor, instance of fragmentation in the story (Saadawi 2018, 242).

The third epigraph is supposedly a quote taken from the Whatsitsname's recording, but curiously, it cannot be found in chapter 10, where his other recordings are collected. The implication, then, is that what is included in the book is just a selection of gathered materials, that no matter how carefully one tries to analyse the story, there will always remain small gaps and incongruencies. The quote contains a direct request to the listeners: "if you don't have the courage to help me with my noble mission, then at least try not to stand in my way." In comparison with the passage from *Frankenstein*, this one is very pragmatic both in form and meaning. The only note of pathos is reserved for the Whatsitsname's "noble mission," which he describes in mystical terms several times in the novel (Saadawi 2018, 142–143, 162). His attitude towards the world, including the people he claims to defend, is disillusioned and not infrequently scornful.

What follows the epigraphs is the List of Characters (in the English edition) and a "Final Report" on the activities of the mysterious Tracking and Pursuit Department. As for the former, Booker and Daraiseh claim it was probably inserted for the convenience of Western readers for whom remembering Arabic names is more difficult (2021), and this is probably true, but it feels very fitting that the list is arranged like a standard Dramatis Personae section at the beginning of a play. It adds another layer of associations to the text and makes Bataween appear almost like a theatre scene, where all the characters "have their exits and their entrances."

The "Final Report" section, on the other hand, is definitely more cryptic than helpful for the reader, who has no idea what this "Tracking and Pursuit Department" is and what it is really responsible for. The report is rather enigmatic and it mentions incidents and people featured in the novel as late as in chapter 18. Labelled as "Top Secret," it intrigues the reader and gives them a sense of being let in on some additional, off the record part of the story. Both the report section and the epigraphs may be classified as belonging to what Genette would call "paratext," a set of elements which despite being located on the periphery of the text, may considerably influence the reader's perception of it (Allen 2006, 103). It is also worth noting that the cover of the English edition – also a part of the paratextual layer – imitates scraps of paper arranged together to make an incongruous picture.

The construction of the novel itself is not less intricate. In fact, it seems even more convoluted, because of how various perspectives intertwine and blend with each other. The book is composed of 19 chapters (and many subchapters) told from numerous different points of view. The main cast includes Elishva, Hadi, Mahmoud al-Sawadi, the Whatsitsname, Brigadier Majid, Faraj the realtor, and Abu Anmar the hotel owner, all of whom are given multiple subchapters. Additionally, there are supporting characters whom the plot follows once or twice, such as Hasib Mohamed Jaafar, Nader Shamouni or the two astrologers employed by Majid. Individual perspectives are stitched together to create a patchwork-like story. For the most part the novel employs third person narration, but the transitions between different points of view are fluent and often blurred. Sometimes typical focalisation is used, as in the case of Elishva's thoughts after the death of Abu Zaidoun (Saadawi 2018, 83)[3] and sometimes the narration remains in the in-between sphere of following the character's perspective without actually filtering the narrative through their consciousness (often Hadi or Mahmoud). It amplifies the atmosphere of general uncertainty and difficulty in establishing the facts.

The collage feel of the plot of *Frankenstein in Baghdad* is further emphasised by the timeline, which frequently moves backwards and forwards and continually poses challenges to the reader who is trying to piece together an organised picture of the occurring events. The most striking example is to be found probably in chapters 16 and 17. The opening of chapter 16 is concerned with Sultan, Saidi's driver; then the narrator moves to Abu Anmar's departure, which had taken place one day earlier, and afterwards to Faraj's perspective to confront the reader with yet another explosion, only to make a step back again and recall events of the previous week, including the arrival of Elishva's grandson and Elishva's decision to finally sell the house and move out of Baghdad – before returning to the moment of the explosion. Minor instances of ambiguity as to the time something happened are virtually omnipresent and make it difficult to construct a coherent timeline. Moreover, the stories of various characters are often inconclusive, left open to interpretation (especially in the cases of Hadi and the Whatsitsname, but of others as well)

---

[3] "There was at least one person who wasn't prepared to make excuses for Abu Zaidoun. Justice at some later stage wouldn't do. It had to happen now. Later there would be time for revenge, for constant torment by a just god, infinite torment, because that's how revenge should be. But justice had to be done here on earth, with witnesses present. Elishva had a vague sense of this when her friend Umm Salim told her in amazement how the wicked old man had been murdered" (Saadawi 2018, 83).

and it is hard to imagine their possible futures, even having read the whole novel.

The feeling of ambiguity and inconclusiveness is additionally strengthened by the uncertainty as to what is "real" and trustworthy. There is a spectrum of "truthfulness" of events: from realistic incidents involving daily life in Bataween, through improbable occurrences such as Hadi gathering fragments of corpses and sewing them together, through supernatural elements lying at the core of the story (the Whatsitsname's existence), to things likely to be rejected entirely, such as St. George speaking from the painting on the wall. It all contributes to the surreal and chaotic atmosphere of the whole novel. The specificity of the wartime setting is yet another aspect of this. Saadawi may use artistic exaggeration to some extent, but in essence, his novel is an authentic reflection of the actual situation. His experience as a reporter, as Alhashmi points out, influenced his literary work, allowing him to capture "the manifold nuances of violence and terror" (2020, 91–92). The continuous flood of violence and the irrational actions of the authorities may, perhaps, seem difficult to imagine to someone who has never experienced living in a country plagued by war, but they are undoubtedly very real to those who have.

Taking into account all those uncertainties and dissonances, the reader may increasingly hesitate as to which version of the events they should believe in. The novel itself playfully points to this problem, as it features many examples of misleading reports or misrepresented facts, urban legends and invented stories. Issues related to authorship and storytelling are brought into focus in a variety of ways.

The "Final Report" in the beginning describes a 17-chapter novel written by "someone referred to as 'the author'" (Saadawi 2018, 2), which apparently could be identified as *Frankenstein in Baghdad* itself, given the context of chapters 18 and 19. But this leads to another problem. *Frankenstein in Baghdad* has 19 chapters. The 18th one is seemingly narrated by this "author" (or "writer") himself, with the use of first person narration, but the 19th chapter employs third person narration again and it includes information which is probably not known to the "author." This raises the question as to who it was that wrote the last chapter. Of course, the reader is aware of the fact that there is a person called Ahmed Saadawi, who *actually* wrote the novel, but the many levels of narration can almost make them forget about this fact – or lose themselves in fantasizing about Saadawi being an "inheritor" of the "author's" work.

In the closing chapters of the novel, the reader finds out that the "author" has talked and exchanged e-mails with Mahmoud, and thus learned the chief parts of Mahmoud's, Hadi's and the Whatsitsname's stories. Apart from that, he apparently sought information from various other characters: "I spent many months visiting Bataween to fill in the other parts of the story. I sat in the coffee shop of Aziz the Egyptian, who said he had visited Hadi in the hospital three times (…) I did get in touch with Father Josiah. I visited him in church and heard from him parts of the story of Elishva, her lost son, her daughters in Australia, and Nader Shamouni the deacon" (Saadawi 2018, 269). This coaxes the reader into accepting the book (at least the first 17 chapters) as his creation. At the same time the whole construction of the novel, numerous shifts between perspectives, and especially the passages which point to the unreliability of storytelling, inevitably make the reader doubt the claims of the "author." To add to the general confusion, the *real* writer's name, "Ahmed Saadawi," sounds suspiciously similar to "Mahmoud al-Sawadi," putting Mahmoud forward as a good candidate for another *alter ego* of Saadawi. The identity of the Whatsitsname may also be doubted, because even though the reader is convinced throughout the plot that he is a real (even if supernatural) character, the "author" claims that the voice from the recordings bears a strong resemblance to the voice of Abu Salim, Hadi's neighbour (Saadawi 2018, 265).

Another metatextual element included in the story is the article Mahmoud writes about the Whatsitsname. He originally gives it the title "Urban Legends from the Streets of Iraq," but Saidi, the owner of the magazine, renames it "Frankenstein in Baghdad," to make it more eye-catching and provocative. Since the whole novel is titled *Frankenstein in Baghdad*, this may well be Saadawi's ironic comment, directed at the publishing industry, as well as at himself. The Whatsitsname is not happy with the published version of his story, as he believes it has portrayed him as a mere sensation and not the hero figure he feels himself to be. Distortion of one's image in the media is, of course, a very real and ubiquitous problem, connected to the broader issue of manipulating available information according to individual or public interest.

Narrative unreliability and the power of words

It is not surprising that narrative unreliability and persuasive power are highlighted in a novel titled after Shelley's *opus magnum*. Let us take a brief look at what and how is achieved in *Frankenstein* in this aspect before comparing it with Saadawi's novel. One of the most recognizable features of *Frankenstein* is its employment of frame narrative, divided between Robert Walton's, Victor Frankenstein's and the creature's points of view, enclosed in one another. Its implications, however, are not always considered. If the reader decides to accept that the novel as a whole is delivered by Robert Walton and thus to treat Victor's and the creature's stories as a kind of extensive quotation, they must face many emerging questions. Should the reader trust that Walton and Victor want to repeat the other stories accurately and truthfully? Their attitudes towards each other are very far from neutral and thus it seems naive to consider them objective listeners and retellers. Walton idolises Victor and does not even try to disguise this fact, openly stating: "My affection for my guest increases every day. He excites at once my admiration and my pity to an astonishing degree" (Shelley 1993, 14). We may therefore assume that he would like to avoid depicting Frankenstein in a bad light, and this may lead him to manipulate the facts which he is recounting. Victor's case is even more problematic, because accepting his point of view as an objective account of events automatically leads to seeing the creature as the antagonist. The reverse is true if we were to see the creature as a reliable narrator, as Eliasson has pointed out (1992, 12). It is only natural that Frankenstein would alter the creature's tale, even if just on the level of style, to avoid portraying him as someone deserving respect and sympathy, as a victim of his own, Victor's, actions. But does Shelley's novel really take this factor into account? Is the reader supposed to assume that the story they are reading has undergone manipulation and that to reach a more truthful picture they should "unfilter" it somehow? This is difficult to determine, especially given that as the stories are told in the novel, the creature's tale definitely *does* portray him as a victim of human aggression, and it does evoke the reader's sympathy.

    Furthermore, although the rhetorical style is comparatively uniform for all three narrative components, some differences still can be discerned. Clark in her analysis of the "protagonism" quality in Shelley's novel proposes a distinction between Walton's, Victor's and the creature's perspectives based on their "capacity for sympathetic identification," the extent to which they are able to understand and describe other characters' personal experience (2014, 246). She believes that this empathic attentiveness which enables one to enter the experience of others is most visible in the creature's account, while often missing in those of Victor and especially Walton (Clark 2014, 245, 249, 257–258). This apparent incongruity may lead the reader to simply forget temporarily about other storytellers and treat each tale separately; or, as Clark proposes, perceive the narrative mode of the novel as a mixture of all three narrators' voices (2014, 253). In the end it is still up to the reader whether they approach Shelley's novel from one specific point of view, or take many of them into account.

Frankenstein in Baghdad does not leave the reader with the same freedom. It frequently reminds the reader of the unreliability of its narratives and narrators, and of the impossibility of reaching the "real" truth. There is one comment made by Mahmoud, which addresses this problem in a very direct way. Before the journalist has the chance to listen to the Whatsitsname's words directly on his recorder, he learns parts of his story from Hadi and he recounts the incident with four beggars in order to preserve it in a digital form: "Mahmoud recorded all this on his digital recorder, aware that he was paraphrasing the words that Hadi had attributed to the Whatsitsname and that he was adding his own personal gloss as well" (Saadawi 2018, 131). On the one hand, this awareness is a sign of the journalist's high sensitivity to words and the power of retelling; on the other hand, it is a straightforward warning against taking any account or story included in the novel for granted.

Saadawi's own meta-textual awareness is amply displayed in this passage as well as many others. Instead of dwelling on each example in detail, I propose a small game very much in the spirit of the novel – stitching together a short text composed exclusively of quotes:

> He sits with us in restaurants, goes into clothing stores, or gets on buses with us, they said. It was an image that had as many forms as there were people to conjure it. Parts of one dream made up for parts missing in another. A little dream filled a gap in a big one, and the threads stitched together. It was anarchy out there; there was no logic behind what was happening.
> Although I had been immersed in this story for a long time, even I started to feel afraid. He fooled me. It was all fantasies and lies. But what if one percent of his story were true? Isn't life a blend of things that are plausible and others that are hard to believe? Today he deceived me and tomorrow I will deceive someone else, also with good intentions. Don't we always do that?
> I'm like the recorder. And as far as I'm concerned, time is like the charge in the battery– not much and not enough. Everything remains half completed.
> I sat in front of my computer and resumed writing. It didn't matter that it was made up.
> (Saadawi 2018, 36, 93, 142, 203, 261, 268, 271, 273, 277)

One cannot help but notice the uncanny relevance which these passages bear towards the construction of *Frankenstein in Baghdad*: they amply display its fragmented narrative, its deliberate mixing of the realistic and the supernatural, and the consciousness of its relationship between the storyteller and the audience.

In fact, many of the characters in the novel are storytellers to various degrees, and the primary example is, of course, Hadi the junk dealer. He is also perfectly conscious of his role and the awareness that literally everything may serve as narrative material never leaves him, even when he is busy with his ordinary work: "Hadi would later narrate these details several times, because he loved details that gave his story credibility and made it more vivid. He would just be telling people about his hard day's work, but they would listen as though it were the best fable Hadi the liar had ever told" (Saadawi 2018, 60). It does not matter that his stories are lies, as long as they are captivating.

Hadi's stories also serve as an additional frame inside the hypothetical "author's" text. On one occasion, the reader follows him during his normal day of visiting potential sellers, and then the perspective shifts to the hotel guard later introduced as Hasib Mohamed Jaafar, only to suddenly break into dialogue: "And now he's going on about the hotel guard!" (Saadawi 2018, 29). It turns out that the whole account was a story narrated by Hadi to his listeners. But was it indeed? Given the style of the passages preceding the dialogue – more literary than casual – this does not seem very probable. And even if a part of it was told as a story, where should the division between Hadi's tale and the exterior narration be made? As was noted in the previous section, Saadawi is blending different perspectives and narrative layers, making his text appear as a kind of living, chaotic entity.

Other characters tell their tales as well. Elishva is known for endlessly reminiscing about her son and she starts to tell "bizarre stories about things that had happened to her" – presumably about the Whatsitsname, or "Daniel" as she calls him (Saadawi 2018, 9); Mahmoud is a journalist, of course; his colleague Farid Shawwaf plans to write an anthology of the one hundred strangest Iraqi stories (Saadawi 2018, 50). Storytellers multiply further: the Whatsitsname records his message, which resembles a report, a confession, and a manifesto at the same time; gossips circling around in Bataween are interesting as well, given how sometimes the "popular version" of certain events may win the admiration of the audience and replace the truth entirely. When one of Elishva's neighbours comes up with a beautiful, touching explanation for the visits of the mysterious man (whom the reader knows to be the Whatsitsname), it does not matter to her listeners that the story is not believable – "it was moving, and the reason they spent part of the day in the courtyard of Umm Salim's house was to escape Bataween and its daily routines and float in another world" (Saadawi 2018, 93). The ability to arrange words in such a way as to entice and influence others is a beautiful gift – but it may also serve as a powerful tool.

The novel frequently tries to make the reader cautious about the power of words and of manipulation. The Whatsitsname is quite frank about it when he describes one of his followers: "The second most important of my assistants is the Sophist, as he calls himself. He's good at explaining ideas, promoting the good ones, polishing them, and making them more powerful. He's good at doing the same for bad ideas too, so he's a man who's dangerous as dynamite." (Saadawi 2018, 145) "Dangerous as dynamite" is not just a literary hyperbole in a book overflowing with accounts of explosions resulting in multiple deaths. The Whatsitsname is completely serious when he emphasises the powerful but treacherous potential of language. He can be quite eloquent himself – he carefully chooses which information to include in his recording and how to present it in order to portray himself as a righteous avenger, instead of a common criminal. His persuasive skills are reflected perhaps a bit humorously in one of his conversations with Hadi:

> "You were just a conduit, Hadi," the Whatsitsname replied. "Think how many stupid mothers and fathers have produced geniuses

and great men in history. The credit isn't due to them but to circumstances and other things beyond their control. You're just an instrument, or a surgical glove that Fate put on its hand to move pawns on the chessboard of life."
Such eloquent talk! Everything Hadi had done – things that no one in his right mind would have undertaken – made him just a conduit, just a paved road that Fate's car could speed along on. (Saadawi 2018, 128)

Another practical example of rhetorical power, as well as manipulative behaviour, is the way Saidi, the magazine owner, maintains his reputation of a successful businessman and becomes a role model for Mahmoud, who imitates his behaviour and dressing style. In the end Saidi is forced to leave Baghdad to avoid being arrested for embezzling thirteen million dollars from the U.S. fund (Saadawi 2018, 252). It is never clearly stated whether he did commit this crime or not, but his treatment of his own employees, whose salaries are left unpaid, is not a good testimony. Nonetheless, when he later sends an email to Mahmoud, trying to persuade the journalist of his innocence, he still manages to cast a hint of doubt in his mind, even leading Mahmoud to hover for a moment "on the verge of apologizing for thinking ill of him" (Saadawi 2018, 277). In the end Mahmoud does not reply to Saidi's message, but even this short period of hesitation demonstrates clearly the dangerous influence of words, especially combined with a charismatic personality.

Persuasive power of rhetoric and deliberate selection of information may have even greater impact when it is employed by official, public media. Saadawi addresses this issue by supplying his novel with multiple instances of propaganda, usually employed by the authorities to conceal their ineffectiveness and inability to tackle the problem of violence in Baghdad. Information turns out to be just a tool, a form of currency. This may remind the reader of the complicated relationship between truth and politics, which is so often defined by antagonism rather than accord. As Arendt points out, even the concept of objective truth is by definition dangerous to those in power, as it represents something that cannot be altered and controlled according to the political interest (2005, 298).

The satire in Saadawi's novel, however, is not directed only against propaganda in the strict sense. Due to its metatextual and linguistic awareness it also unmasks the selectivity and self-interest driving all interpretative effort. One comment concerning Saidi's "political friends" is particularly interesting here: "They look at the Tracking and Pursuit Department (...) as if they're looking at a text–each party interprets it according to its own interest." (Saadawi 2018, 178). The presupposition here is that even the act of reading involves some level of manipulation, and this may be applied not only to political contexts, but also to research in general, and literary studies in particular.

Naturally, this emphasis on the relativity of truth contributes to the postmodern quality of Saadawi's novel. After all, one of the recognizable features of postmodern philosophy and fiction is the insistence on subjectivity and rejection of the possibility of acquiring certain knowledge about reality (Duignan 2020). On the one hand, this may be an inspiring phenomenon, but on the other – as Kakutani, among others, points out – it may lead to a disturbing level of disregard for the facts. She argues that there are many who "exploited the postmodernist argument that all truths are partial," creating implausible, controversial alternative histories (Kakutani 2018, 55–56). *Frankenstein in Baghdad*, being a very self-aware novel, forces the reader to face the complexity and chaos of different perspectives and agendas, but at the same time warns them against believing anyone's "subjective truth."

Conclusion

Although it may appear chaotic and hard to navigate at first, *Frankenstein in Baghdad* is actually "a highly self-conscious, highly *constructed* literary text, very much in the mode of so many works of Western postmodernism" (Booker and Daraiseh 2021), in which the form and the content remain inseparable and echo each other, foregrounding the recurrent motifs of fragmentation, incongruity and uncertainty. On the level of the plot and setting it draws attention to the reality of terror and violence pervading the streets of Baghdad, the cruel ubiquity of bodies ripped to pieces, and the overwhelming anxiety of living in times of modern military conflict. The narrative and structural layer emphasise the surreal and fragmentary sense of reality and the difficulty of establishing any certain facts when faced with a plethora of perspectives and increasingly questionable occurrences. Storytelling frames and metatextual comments serve to raise the reader's awareness of the unreliable nature of all narration and the manipulative power of language. Saadawi may have borrowed the concept of an artificially assembled body from Mary Shelley's *Frankenstein*, but he pushes the themes of vengeance and (in)justice, as well as the relativity of subjective truth, into a very different territory, not just in terms of the sociopolitical context of post-2003 Iraq, but also the broad panorama of contemporary global problems. Incredibility of information, contradictory messages in public media, unpredictability of everyday existence and, perhaps the most tragically, instrumentalization and lack of respect towards human bodies and lives, are acutely felt in many, if not all, countries across the world. *Frankenstein in Baghdad* is both an impressive literary accomplishment and a deeply insightful, socially committed project.

References

Abdalkafor, Ola. 2018. "Frankenstein and Frankenstein in Baghdad: The Sovereign, Homo Sacer and Violence." *Postcolonial Text* 13(3). https://www.postcolonial.org/index.php/pct/article/view/2365/2213 (accessed 23 June 2023).

Alhashmi, Rawad. 2020. "The Grotesque in Frankenstein in Baghdad: Between Humanity and Monstrosity." *International Journal of Language and Literary Studies* 2(1), 90–106. https://doi.org/10.36892/ijlls.v2i1.120

Allen, Graham. 2006. *Intertextuality*. London and New York. Routledge. https://ia902808.us.archive.org/4/items/AllenGraham2000Intertextuality/Allen%2C%20Graham%20%282000%29%20Intertextuality.pdf (accessed 23 June 2023).

Arendt, Hannah. 2005. "Truth and Politics." In: *Truth. Engagements Across Philosophical Traditions*. Eds. José Medina and David Wood. Malden. Blackwell Publishing, 295–314.

Bahoora, Haytham. 2015. "Writing the Dismembered Nation: The Aesthetics of Horror in Iraqi Narratives of War." *The Arab Studies Journal* 23(1), 184–208. http://www.jstor.org/stable/44744904

Booker, M. Keith and Isra Daraiseh. 2021. "Frankenstein in Baghdad, or the Postmodern Prometheus." *Comments on Culture*. https://bookerhorror.com/frankenstein-in-baghdad-or-the-postmodern-prometheus/ (accessed 23 June 2023).

Clark, Anne E. 2014. "*Frankenstein*; or, the Modern Protagonist." *ELH* 81(1), 245–268. http://www.jstor.org/stable/24475594

Cottom, Daniel. 1980. "Frankenstein and the Monster of Representation." *SubStance* 9(3) (1980), 60–71. https://doi.org/10.2307/3683905

Duignan, Brian. 2020. "Postmodernism." *Encyclopédia Britannica*. https://www.britannica.com/topic/postmodernism-philosophy (accessed 23 June 2023).

Eliasson, Albin. 1992. "Monstrous Truths and Hidden Lies: A Reading of *Frankenstein*'s Narrative Structure and its Effects." Örebro University. https://www.diva-portal.org/smash/get/diva2:918012/FULLTEXT01.pdf (accessed 23 June 2023).

Kakutani, Michiko. 2018. *The Death of Truth: Notes on Falsehood in the Age of Trump*. New York. Tim Duggan Books.

Murphy, Sinéad. 2018. "*Frankenstein in Baghdad*: Human Conditions, or Conditions of Being Human." *Science Fiction Studies* 45(2), 273–288. https://doi.org/10.5621/sciefictstud.45.2.0273

Saadawi, Ahmed. 2018. *Frankenstein in Baghdad*. Translated by Jonathan Wright. New York. Penguin Books.

Shelley, Mary. 1993. *Frankenstein*. Ed. Marilyn Butler. London. Pickering & Chatto.

Vargo, Lisa. 2016. "Contextualizing Sources." In: *The Cambridge Companion to Frankenstein*. Ed. Andrew Smith. Cambridge. Cambridge University Press, 26–32.

Anna Kwiatek

3.
"'Twixt my extremes and me this bloody knife / Shall play the umpire": Suicide (Not) Romanticised in *Romeo and Juliet* and *Hamlet*

Introduction

In one of the prefaces to John Sym's *Lifes Preservative Against Self-Killing*, William Gouge makes the following comment on suicide: "I suppose, that scarce an age since the beginning of the world hath afforded more examples of this desperate inhumanity, than this our present age" (Gouge 1637). Although barely anyone would describe the act as "inhumane" now, 400 years later, the sentiment remains the same. There is just one fundamental difference: now we have more reliable data to support such a claim. According to WHO, at least 700 000 people die by suicide every year (2021). It has been identified as the fourth leading cause of death among 15–29-year-olds worldwide. Between the years 2001 and 2020, suicide was among the top ten leading causes of death for individuals of all age groups, and the second leading cause of death among 25–34-year-olds in the US (Centers for Disease Control and Prevention 2023). With such drastic numbers, concerns have been raised about potential contributing factors, among them the influence of media. Consequently, in 2017 WHO released guidelines for media reporting of suicides in an attempt to mitigate the damage done by reckless journalism.

Fictitious representations of suicide have undergone nearly the same degree of scrutiny as reports of real deaths. In March 2017 a television series called *13 Reasons Why* was released on Netflix. The show partly aimed to raise awareness about mental health. However, it quickly got infamous for its detailed and highly graphic portrayal of the suicide of the main character, Hannah, and the unusual degree of control over the narrative she exerts even after her death. Zoe Williams from *The Guardian* wrote: "if there was a list of ways not to portray suicide, this would tick every box (…). It normalises and legitimises the act. It goes into too much and too graphic detail about the suicide itself" (2017). Likewise, on CNN, Mark Henick voiced the opinion that the series' "narrative choice, while an artistic one, is also a potentially devastating setback in the effort to combat a problem which by any conservative estimate is a global health crisis" (2017).

The controversy prompted a new direction in the discussion: a potential link between showing suicide as part of a creative story and actual suicides happening in the real world. Recent studies show that the idea of the existence of such a connection might be more than just pure speculation. Within 19 days of the release of *13 Reasons Why*, Google searches for suicide-related queries increased by

19%, as the series "increased suicide awareness while unintentionally increasing suicidal ideation" (Ayers et al. 2017, 1528–1529). A study conducted in 2019 notes a 13.3% increase in the number of suicides in the US among the show's target audience of 10–19-year-olds within the first three months after its release, while less vulnerable age groups seem to have been less affected (Niederkrotenthaler et al. 2019, 937). While, as the authors of the study themselves protest, this does not ultimately confirm a causal relationship between the series and suicidal deaths, the results are too alarming for such a possibility to be ignored.

Among numerous accusations and grievances raised against *13 Reasons Why* was the claim that it "romanticised" suicide. To give but one of many examples, Ged Flynn from a charity dealing with suicide prevention warned the potential viewers to "be aware that when watching this programme there is a danger that suicide is romanticised and sensationalised" (Campbell 2017). Since the word "to romanticise" itself may sound a bit vague, and its meaning is often blurred in those discussions, it will be useful to first define it. According to the Oxford English Dictionary, the transitive verb "to romanticise" means "[t]o make romantic or idealized in character; to make (something) seem better or more appealing than it really is; to describe, portray, or view in a romantic manner." The word "romantic" in this definition could be conceived as ambiguous. Nevertheless, given that the entry author uses "idealized" as a synonym, it is relatively safe to assume that the sense in which the word is used here is "sentimental." Regardless, it is not only *13 Reasons Why* and other television shows that have been criticised for using this specific word. The term "romanticising" has frequently been used in discussions about the portrayal of sensitive content in both visual arts and literature. One only has to perform a quick Google search to find articles like "'All the Bright

Places:' A brief interlude on romanticizing suicide" on the Chatham University community blog, or discussion threads like "Is this book romanticizing suicide?" on the Goodreads page for a book entitled *Beautiful Broken Girls*.

It is not just modern creative works that have been disparaged for misrepresenting suicide as well as other difficult themes. Similar accusations have been fired towards the numerous products of past ages, especially the classics. Shakespeare, as one of the few truly ubiquitous authors in the Western canon, has understandably been one of the primary targets of criticism, especially on the web. The first response in a recent Reddit thread entitled "Stop romanticizing suicide" is "romeo and juliet is the definition of this," to which another user teasingly replies "It was a very romantic suicide ;)" (2023). Those opinions tend to be conveyed in a rather minimalistic and generalised way. This is partly due to the conventions and limitations of communication on social media, which is where they are often expressed. There is also a focus on the plot and what is being either said or shown, whereas how it is being said is rarely taken into consideration.

There is little to no involvement from academics in the debate. There is, of course, scholarship dealing with difficult themes in Shakespeare, among them suicide,[1] but it does not really acknowledge them as being such from the reader's/audience's perspective and therefore deserving of special consideration. The very few papers that are of any relevance deal with issues such as whether we need trigger warnings for difficult content in general and why (see

---

[1] See Rowland Wymer's *Suicide and Despair in the Jacobean Drama* (1986); Eric Langley's *Narcissism and Suicide in Shakespeare and His Contemporaries* (2009), Marlena Tronicke's *Shakespeare's Suicides: Dead Bodies That Matter* (2018) or Drew Daniel's *Joy of the Worm* (2022).

Kirsten Mendoza's "Sexual Violence, Trigger Warnings, and the Early Modern Classroom" (2019)) or with the presence of Shakespeare on the web and social media in general, e.g., Stephen O'Neill's *Shakespeare and Youtube* (2014). The first category, although much needed, shifts the focus to how or whether to deal with such content at all, and does not give due diligence to how exactly it is dramatized in Shakespeare, and what aspects of its presentation might make it more or less "triggering" than the treatment of similar themes in other works of literature. The present chapter is an attempt to nurture a budding scholarly angle in the already existing popular discussion on the specifics of difficult themes in Shakespeare by taking a closer look at whether Shakespeare romanticises suicidal death in his plays, and if so, to what extent. More specifically, I intend to argue that while in my chosen plays there are instances where suicidal death is elevated, the works viewed in their entirety do not romanticise it. The plays *Romeo and Juliet* and *Hamlet*, have been singled out for the analysis mainly on the basis of how often they tend to be brought up in the internet discourse. Following the Oxford English Dictionary definition, in the texts I analyse, I will pay special attention to any signs of suicide nostalgia, its elevation and idealisation in order to determine how they fit into a larger narrative concerning the representation of suicide within the chosen dramatic texts.

Romeo and Juliet's "timeless end"

It has been noted many times that *Romeo and Juliet* is like a comedy gone awry. Up to a point, we witness a pair of secret lovers, meeting against the will of their families, enthralled by each other's affection.

But the deaths of Tybalt and Mercutio mark the play's switch from comedy to tragedy, starting a stream of misfortunes which bring the young lovers to an untimely death. Nonetheless, a strong sense of foreboding is present in the play from the outset. Through the Prologue it is made clear that the story is going to have a tragic ending, that the amorous passion is to end with death: "From forth the fatal loins of these two foes / A pair of star-crossed lovers take their life" (Prologue 1–2) and their love is "death-marked" (5). What can feel even more eerie is that even Romeo and Juliet themselves have a sense of something bad that is bound to happen and result in their deaths. Right before meeting Juliet for the first time, Romeo feels that he will be overcome by "some vile forfeit of untimely death" (1.4.11) unless some grand force decides otherwise (112–113). After the wedding night, Juliet exclaims to Romeo, who has just gone out of her chamber and is climbing down the ladder: "O God, I have an ill-divining soul! / Methinks I see thee now, thou art so low, / As one dead in the bottom of a tomb (3.5.51–53).

On the other hand, independently from that sense of incoming calamity, the lovers themselves assert many times throughout the play that untimely death is preferable to a long life without each other's affections. This starts on a metaphorical level, with readiness to give up familial name and identity ("Call me but love and I'll be new baptized. / Henceforth I never will be Romeo" (2.2.47–51)) and quickly moves onto a more literal willingness to die: "My life were better ended by their hate / Than death prorogued, wanting of thy love" (77–78). After meeting Romeo for the first time, Juliet says: "If he be married, / My grave is like to be my wedding bed" (1.4.133–34), and a similar sentiment is repeated in 3.2 (I'll to my wedding bed / And death, not Romeo, take my maidenhead (96–137)), as well as in 3.5 ((...) make the bridal bed / In that dim monument where Tybalt lies

(201–202)). On a basic level, those words would mean that Juliet is not willing to consummate her relationship with anyone else than Romeo; however, they also imply that she would prefer to die rather than do it. Thus, the main characters frame death as a desirable way out of the obligations bestowed upon them by their families: it has the power to save them from unhappy life.

When the lovers first become suicidal, it is a movement from that preference for death to the straightforward "either we are together or I die" sentiment which admits no compromises but is in line with the youth of the main characters. After the death of Tybalt, the Nurse comes to bring Juliet the news of his demise and Romeo's banishment. She is, however, too distracted by the shocking turn of events to get straight to the point of what has happened, which provokes Juliet's impatience and she passionately exclaims: "Hath Romeo slain himself? Say thou but 'Ay', / And that bare vowel 'I' shall poison more (...) I am not I if there be such an 'Ay'" (3.2.45–46; 48). Contemplating the possibility of Romeo's death, Juliet immediately thinks of killing herself. It is also telling that the first cause of his death that she can think of is suicide.

Likewise, having been sentenced to banishment, Romeo quickly concludes that death would be better than separation from his beloved: "Ha, banishment? Be merciful, say 'death'" (3.3.12). Having heard from the Nurse about Juliet's grief, he attempts to stab himself, but is restrained by Friar Laurence, whose scolding is prolonged to the extent that it becomes comical: the godly man speaks 51 verse lines straight. The Friar accuses Romeo of desperation, effeminacy, being overcome by emotion and not keeping his passion moderate, selfishness, disrespect for the natural order, wasting his own intelligence, physical fitness and general potential to do good (107–157). Jill L. Levenson points out that the speech "illustrates one of Shakespeare's straightforward techniques for calling rhetoric into question: setting an accomplished performance into a context which reduces its effect" (1996, 49). I would add that apart from the sheer number of faults Friar Laurence finds with Romeo's actions, some rhetorical devices he uses inadvertently contribute to the comic effect. For example, there are numerous repetitions and at the same time tricolon lists, such as "Why rail'st thou on thy birth, the heaven and earth, / Since birth, and heaven, and earth, all three do meet / In thee at once" (118–120) or "Fie, fie, thou sham'st thy shape, thy love, thy wit, (...)/ Which should bedeck thy shape, thy love, thy wit" (121; 24). Thus, the effect of the Friar's speech is that it dissolves the tension produced by Romeo's hasty suicidal attempt and ridicules it by contrasting Romeo's elevated tone of speech. On the other hand, the Friar himself also comes across as funny, and his arguments against suicide are undermined by his chaotic rhetoric. The gravity of Romeo's passionate upheaval, however, is in consequence dissipated, an effect which is amplified by the reader's or audience's memory of his too easily cured despair over the earlier love interest Rosaline in 1.1.

The situation is mirrored by the more serious conversation Juliet has with Friar Laurence after she has learned she had to marry Paris. This time, neither of the speakers dominates the conversation and the tone is more solemn. Juliet is determined to find a way out of her upcoming marriage to Paris, whether it is by the Friar's cunning or by death: "Give me some present counsel, or behold, / 'Twixt my extremes and me this bloody knife / Shall play the umpire" (4.1.61–63); "I long to die, / If what thou speak'st speak not of remedy" (66–67). The offered solution, the sleeping draught, is to produce a mock-version of what Juliet would have done otherwise; not only of death in general, but also of suicide. To Friar Laurence, it "craves as desperate an execution / As that is desperate which we would prevent" (69–70). It is "a thing like death (...) / That cop'st with death himself to scape from it" (74–75).

The Friar's reasoning contains traces of the early modern discourse on suicide: in the *Anatomy of Melancholy* Burton describes suicide as a paradox of "dying to escape death" (2022, 437) and the idea, likely taken from St. Augustine, is present in some other early modern texts as well. What also draws attention is the repetition of the word "desperate," also repeated by the Friar in his scolding of Romeo in 3.3. In 3.3.63, in the Folio text of the play, the Friar says he will "dispaire" instead of "dispute" with Romeo (1623, 67 sig. ff4$_r$), which grants him yet another repetition of the word. While there is no guarantee that this word is what was originally in either the authorial manuscript or the play's performance, it still does say something about how whoever caused it to be in there saw Romeo's plight. Despair in the religious sense is something which may mean little to us, but for Shakespeare's contemporaries, it was perceived as strongly connected to suicide and especially relevant for those scenes (Wymer 1986, 22).

Juliet's speech before taking the sleeping draught (4.3.15–59) reveals the extent of her anxiety about the failure of the scheme. She is worried that the potion will not work at all, that it is a disguised poison, that Romeo will come too late, or that she will go mad from lying beside the dead and kill herself. Her family's burial monument is here a grim and sinister place, housing the corpse of "bloody Tybalt" (42), and nightly "spirits" (44) and where one can hear "shrieks like mandrakes torn out of the earth" (47). At the same time, she is determined to take the risk and to deal with any negative outcomes. She reasserts that if the draught does not work, she can still kill herself in order not to marry Paris (21–23). It is interesting that in the same speech, in two different contexts, Juliet comforts herself with the possibility of killing herself and is horrified by it. Her fears, however, seem to mostly concern the lack of control over her own body which is an inevitable part of taking the draught, and that it might end up in her going insane. Therefore suicide, depending on the degree of her own agency in it, is the ultimate way of avoiding re-marrying and thus staying faithful to her husband, or a dreadful manifestation of madness.

Romeo's reaction to Juliet's supposed "death" is creating a scheme for his own: "Well, Juliet, I will lie with thee tonight. / Let's see for means. O mischief, thou art swift / To enter in the thoughts of desperate men" (5.1.34–36), he says, off to buy poison. By the time he has approached the Capulet monument, he is distraught and emotionally unstable to the point of the release of his animal instincts. He threatens to "tear" Balthazar "joint by joint" (5.3.35) if he interrupts the hero's "savage-wild" intents in any way (37). This threat is materialised when Romeo sees Paris, who blames him for Juliet's death and wants to capture him. He tells Paris to "tempt not a desperate man" (59) and reveals his suicidal intent to the rival ("I love thee better than myself, / For I come hither armed against myself (64–65)) and urges him to leave. Paris, however, has no intention of doing so, and so is killed by Romeo. Romeo's "wildness" and violence is further emphasised by the prying tools he carries for the purpose of opening the tomb: a mattock and a crow, which symbolise "breaking open what should be inviolate and thrusting both himself and, unknowingly, Juliet into the maw of death" (Dessen 1995, 194).

There is a multitude of critical conceptions as to why the play's eponymous characters kill themselves and what this means, assigning to them different degrees of agency in deciding their fate. Most critics tend to view the lovers as at least to some extent triumphant in the scene. In fact, one might wonder whether the critical inclination to idealise the lovers has had any impact on modern accusations that the play romanticises their deaths. T.J. Cribb (1982) and Kathleen E. McLuskie (1971) exemplify the idealistic view of Romeo and Juliet's deaths: their last moments are "distinctively ideal, emotional and unnaturalistic" (Cribb 1982, 96); they "achieve a glory denied to the exponents of the world of sense" (McLuskie 1971, 69). In Julia Kristeva's psychoanalytical reading, the lovers' desire is a destructive force in itself, bound to either extinguish or lead to death (1987, 214, 222). "If marriage is wedded to passion," Kristeva writes, "how could it last without some rehabilitation of perversion?" (1987, 217. For her, the intense relationship of Macbeth and the Lady in *Macbeth* is its prime example and she claims that Shakespeare "saved" Romeo and Juliet's purity by having them kill themselves (1987, 217). Levenson similarly highlights the tradition of *Liebestod*, where "the compulsion to love is a compulsion to die, and death is the price for an absolute" (2000, 46); however, for Levenson this is just one of multiple narratives present in the play and her view is less deterministic. To Coppélia Kahn, for the lovers "death is a transcendent form of sexual consummation" and "rebirth into a higher stage of existence" which at the same time allows them to achieve maturity. There is no compulsion in her view: "love-death is not merely fated; it is willed" and their suicide "is the lovers' triumphant assertion over the (…) world which has kept them apart" (1977, 19).

Hugh Grady contests the idea of *Liebestod*'s relevance to the play, arguing that desire in *Romeo and Juliet* is presented as the opposite of death rather than connected with it (2009). The play "create[s] kinetic dialectics between death and desire, in which each of these human basics asserts its triumph and then its defeat in endless aesthetic oscillation;" it "represents the defeat of death by desire crystallized in art at the same time that it recognizes and mourns both the cruelty of chance and the inevitability of death" (Grady 2009, 203–204). Paul A. Kottman, inspired by Georg W.F. Hegel, argues that the lovers' suicides are a final act in their struggle for self-realisation through the mutual recognition of each other as an individual, which requires them to stake their lives (2012). Ewan Fernie draws from this interpretation, but at the same time he points out the social dimension of the deaths, which is downplayed by Kottman (2017).

Other critics are slightly more sceptical concerning the lovers' agency and/or capacity for judgement. In her materialist, determinist reading, Susan Snyder argues that the feud as the all-pervasive force creating the play's sociopolitical reality can be viewed as akin to ideology in the Althusserian sense. Therefore, ultimately Romeo and Juliet are left "with nowhere to go, nothing to do except die" because for "individuals who try to advance beyond their ideology but cannot undo its constitutive influence, there is no feasible way to live (Snyder 1995, 93). Crawford argues that "[w]e may wish to see their suicides as defiant acts that preserve the purity of their love, but the play shows death itself as triumphant," pointing to the presence of Paris in the tomb and inverted feasting imagery in Romeo's speech (2015, 228, 333). John Kleiner, in turn, argues that Romeo is self-deceiving in the tomb: he chooses to ignore the signs that Juliet is alive and opts out of the possible comic ending for the play (2014).

The critics dealing specifically with Shakespearean suicides are better at capturing the ambivalence of the lovers' deaths. Rowland Wymer frames Romeo and Juliet's deaths within the tradition of love-suicides; death is an obstacle but at the same time "the end of all obstruction and hence the attainment of a union which would be impossible on earth" (1986, 112). Still, to Wymer, the play subtly acts out the tension between the religious and the romantic understanding of suicide, and "although it requires a peculiar insensitivity to the tone of the play to regard the lovers as guilty sinners, it is true that the spectre of Despair hovers in the background in various key moments" (116). The lovers' deaths are "free from the *guilt* of the despair implied here, but not its bitterness" and "[t]heir suicides lead them neither to hell nor a lovers' heaven but only to a dark and silent, though shared, tomb" (117).

Tronicke (2018), in turn, thinks that "the portrayal of Romeo and Juliet's suicides works against the play's self-constructed ethos of undying, romantic love" and that their death scene "toys with tragedy's generic boundaries (...) because gendered expectations regarding traditionally masculine and feminine deaths are reversed" (35). This reversal prompts us to admire Juliet and limits the sympathy for her beloved. Tronicke sees Romeo, as opposed to the more rational Juliet, as starkly defined by his status as a Petrarchan lover, who longs for death, masochistically finding pleasure in rejection and (non-religious) despair. He is forced to curb this side of him when he enters into the relationship with Juliet. However, inside the Capulet tomb, it resurfaces: "death has taken Juliet, and so his desire will ultimately remain unfulfilled" (41). Romeo's highly conventional language alienates him from the audience (42). Tronicke points out Romeo's use of poison, a traditionally feminine means of death (40) and Juliet's failed attempt at gathering some of it from her lover's lips: "figuratively speaking, the gentler weapon poison may kill the weak Romeo but is not strong enough to kill the stronger Juliet" (44). In dying by a blade, the means traditionally associated with Roman suicide, she dies more "masculine" than Romeo (45).

I opt for a nuanced view of the death scene. Like the rest of the play, it revels in contrast and paradox. Having just violently killed Paris, Romeo goes on to peacefully admire the sight of Juliet in her grave, whose beauty is put against the darkness and terror of the monument:

A grave – O, no, a lantern, slaughtered youth,
For here lies Juliet, and her beauty makes
This vault a feasting presence full of light.
Death, lie thou there, by a dead man interred (5.3.84–87).

Despite the apparent intimacy of the moment, Crawford draws attention to the often dismissed (or altogether erased in performance) continuing presence of Paris' dead body. Juliet's former suitor is likely laid close to her, and there is no reason to suppose him absent from the scene when the lovers kill themselves, which makes their last moments less private than one would like to think (2015, 323). He also notes the ubiquity of death in this scene: the tomb, the supposedly, and then actually, dead Juliet, Paris killed, Tybalt buried there, and finally Romeo who addresses Death and calls himself a "dead man" before taking his life. Lastly, it is marked by the presence of worms (109) which "emblematize the processes of decomposition, and thus death's power of indistinction" (328, 338).

Nonetheless, the vault is also full of life, though shadowed by death: Romeo sees himself as a person who experiences a surge of life right before his death ("How oft, when men are at the point of death, / Have they been merry, which their keepers call / A lightening before death" 5.3.88–90). Juliet has not been "conquered" (94) by death, because she is still beautiful: her cheeks are red, full of life: "Thou art not conquered. Beauty's ensign yet / Is crimson in thy lips and in thy cheeks, / And death's pale flag is not advanced there" (93–96). All this is of course, ironic, because Juliet is not dead and Romeo does not realise that. Romeo notices Tybalt's grave and the "lifelike" redness of Juliet's skin for an instant becomes the bloody red of a killed young man ("Tybalt, liest thou there in thy bloody sheet?" (97)).

Romeo's suicide is that of a lover. The "dead" Juliet is also described as a lover: however, instead of loving Romeo, she has been forced to become the lover of personified Death, who has replaced her rightful husband ("That unsubstantial death is amorous, / And that the lean abhorred monster keeps / Thee here in dark to be his paramour?" (103–105)). To save and protect her from Death's embrace, Romeo is going to join her. The poison he drinks is a toast to Juliet ("Here's to my love" (119)), whose body he then embraces and kisses (113–114), inadvertently becoming just the personified Death figure he sought to free her from. Romeo also sees his suicide as a way to get rid of the adverse fate to which he is doomed: "shake the yoke of inauspicious stars" (111). He does not recognise, however, that by killing himself he is fulfilling the very destiny that has been set for him. Although one might hope for a different ending until the last minute, within the world of this play, there is nothing more predictable than the suicides of Romeo and Juliet.

If Romeo's death is utterly tragic and full of dramatic irony, his dying speech is nevertheless an aesthetically pleasant piece of poetry, and a good base for an actor to show off their skill. Metrically, the speech is carefully crafted. Iambs sometimes give way to trochees or even spondees, especially in line beginnings, to add momentum and underscore the gravity of the moment. The perfect pentameter, however, is maintained throughout, with only a few exceptions, lines 93, 101, 116 and 119, which mark important transitions that could be a clue for the actor to change pace or show emotion.

Soon after Romeo has died, Friar Laurence comes in and Juliet wakes up from her faux death. Seeing her husband's dead body, she ignores the Friar's pleas to leave with him: just as for Romeo, for her life without her love would have been pointless. Her suicide speech is much more concise than Romeo's. Just like him, she wants to die "with a kiss." However, the kiss is not enough to kill, and, upon hearing some commotion outside, she quickly takes up a dagger to then stab herself. In some of Shakespeare's works, the prolonging of a suicidal death has a palpable comic effect, a prominent example being Anthony's death in *Antony and Cleopatra*. This does not seem to be the case here. Instead, it builds suspense on the one hand, as we are not sure whether Juliet will manage to kill herself before someone comes in, and in this climactic moment we sympathise with her plight. The difficulty, on the other hand, of having to kill herself by other means makes the situation more tragic and less picturesque, as well as showing Juliet's determination. While killing herself, she acts out the earlier, consistent preference for death over life without Romeo and there is a sense of triumph in this consistency.

The dead couple is discovered by watchmen and, although the lovers framed their deaths as stemming from the pursuit of private, intimate feeling, there seems to be much public outrage and mourning for them: "O, the people in the street cry 'Romeo,' / Some 'Juliet,' and some 'Paris', and all run / With open outcry toward our monument" (5.3.191–193). Thus after their death, the couple receives a degree of public attention they never had during life. Death is brought to the forefront: the Chief Watchman's account, the word "dead" is repeated: "And Romeo dead, and Juliet, dead before, / Warm and new killed" (196–197). Capulet's Wife calls the lovers a "sight of death" (206), just before Montague announces that his "wife is dead tonight" (210). Friar Laurence soon begins his account of the events by explaining that "Romeo, there dead, was husband to that Juliet, / And she, there dead, that's Romeo's faithful wife" (31–32). Having heard the entire story, the Prince frames the lovers' deaths as a divine punishment for the feud: "See what a scourge is laid upon your hate, / That heaven finds means to kill your joys with love" (292–293), and the grieving heads of the two houses make up beside their dead children's bodies. Finally acknowledging Romeo and Juliet's affection, they vow to honour their respective children-in-law by raising statues to them.

The play is concluded by one last speech of the Prince, where he acknowledges the bittersweet new beginning: "a glooming peace" (305), and brings the dead lovers to the forefront again, saying that "never was a story of more woe, / Than this of Juliet and her Romeo" (309–310). Thus, on the one hand, the lovers' death is portrayed as a clearly tragic event for both families and the community, a "punishment" for the endless feud. On the other hand, their tragic death is portrayed as inevitable for the feud to end. The peace would not have been possible had Romeo and Juliet not died like they did.

The dead couple's elevation into a statue is a final acknowledgment of their love, and honours their suicidal death, attempting to erase its negative influence by immortalising them in the form of art. This could be seen as a glorification of their suicides: not only is Juliet and Romeo's relationship recognised after they have killed themselves, but they also make an impact on the entire community and are mythologised as statues for future generations to behold. Immortalised in this way, they hold more power and agency within their community than they ever had before. Nonetheless, the play provides a hint that such a perception of the ending might be misguided. After making a handsome payment to the apothecary who would otherwise be reluctant to sell him poison, Romeo remarks: "There is thy gold, worse poison o men's souls, / Doing more murder in this loathsome world / Than these poor compounds that thou mayst not sell" (5.1.80–82). The gold that enabled his tragic death is now replaced by the gold which is going to give him a new life in the form of a statue: or is it?

The doubtful deaths of *Hamlet*

Of all Shakespeare's works, *Hamlet* is the play most associated with suicide, even though it is not the one with the most suicidal deaths. In fact, discussion remains as to whether there are any suicides at all. Arguably, the most suicide-like death is this of Ophelia. Violently pushed away by Hamlet and mourning the death of her father, she sinks into madness and drowns (herself). The principal counterclaim is that there is no explicit statement in the play that Ophelia killed herself and her death is not shown onstage. What we have is a witness's account which suggests accidental death, and an assumption of suicide by two grave-makers, followed by an incomplete funerary rite and a priest who strongly suspects self-killing. Suicide, however, is to me the most logical explanation of Ophelia's death. The account which highlights Ophelia's lack of agency belongs to a person with potential bias: Gertrude, while the opinion that her death is suicide is given by strangers, which could make it more objective. Furthermore, according to MacDonald, the death of an insane person by suicide would have been more likely to be ruled an accident in an effort to protect the deceased rather than *non compos mentis*, which was a very rare verdict and an option likely unknown by most (1986, 313). Gertrude's account could be seen as an example of such attempt to maintain Ophelia's reputation. Moreover, viewing her death as suicide is much more dramatically compelling (Tronicke 2018, 78–82), as it provides a contrast for Hamlet's unfulfilled suicidal musings.

Ophelia's madness is shown as pitiful and beautiful at the same time: watching her give away flowers, her brother comments that "Thought and afflictions, passion, hell itself / She turns to favour and to prettiness" (4.5.180–81). A similar thing can be said about her suicide, which is on the one hand a tragic event, yet her dead body is portrayed as pleasant to behold. Gertrude's speech (4.7.64–81) is very lyrical, laden with nature imagery, and evokes a pastoral, which is incongruous with an account of a sudden and tragic death.

> There is a willow grows askant the brook
> That shows his hoary leaves in the glassy stream.
> Therewith fantastic garlands did she make
> Of crowflowers, nettles, daisies and long purples,
> That liberal shepherds give a grosser name
> But our cold maids do dead men's fingers call them.
> There on the pendent boughs her crownet weeds
> Clambering to hang, an envious sliver broke,
> When down her weedy trophies and herself
> Fell in the weeping brook. Her clothes spread wide
> And mermaid-like awhile they bore her up,
> Which time she chanted snatches of old lauds
> As one incapable of her own distress,
> Or like a creature native and endued
> Unto that element. But long it could not be
> Till that her garments, heavy with their drink,
> Pulled the poor wretch from her melodious lay
> To muddy death. (4.7.164–81)

The description with its willow tree on the one hand gestures towards Ovid's ideal place (Macfie 2022, 242). On the other hand, the willow was commonly used as a symbol of unrequited love (Shakespeare 2016, 437), which frames Ophelia as an abandoned lover. This is especially interesting if one considers Polonius's words from 2.1, where he says that love's "violent property fordoes itself / And leads the will to desperate undertakings" (100–101). Little did Polonius know at the moment that his words were more accurate as a description of his daughter's behaviour than Hamlet's.

Ophelia's agency in Gertrude's account is removed and her death here feels like an accident or even murder by the "envious sliver" (171). Her beauty and grace are elevated by the comparison to a mythological creature: her clothes are of a "mermaid-like" (174) shape. While there is a sense of sympathy and recognition of her woe in this account, it is not a dominating force. The "weeping brook," although in contrast with Ophelia's blissful unawareness of her own tragedy, is overshadowed by the emergent image of a boundless mythologized figure. The painful process of dying itself is omitted. The picture is one of a suicide elevated to a thing of beauty, in which a carefree, innocent maid achieves a quasi-mystical communion with nature.

Unlike Gertrude, who in her flowery speech is hesitant to name Ophelia as an agent of her own death, the gravediggers we meet in 5.1 have no qualms about laying it bare, or even joking about the extent of her agency.

> GRAVEDIGGER Is she to be buried in Christian burial, when she wilfully seeks her own salvation?
> 2 MAN I tell thee she is. Therefore make her grave straight. The crowner hath sat on her and finds it Christian burial.
> GRAVEDIGGER How can that be unless she drowned

> herself in her own defence?
> 2 MAN Why, 'tis found so.
> (...)
> GRAVEDIGGER Give me leave. Here lies the water – good.
> Here stands the man – good. If the man go to this water
> and drown himself, it is, willy-nilly, he goes. Mark you
> that. But if the water come to him and drown him, he
> drowns not himself. Argal, he that is not guilty of his
> own death shortens not his own life.
> 2 MAN But is this law?
> GRAVEDIGGER Ay, marry is't. Crowner's 'quest law.
> 2 MAN Will you ha' the truth on't? If this had not been a
> gentlewoman she should have been buried out o' Christian
> burial.
> GRAVEDIGGER Why, there thou sayst, and the more pity
> that great folk should have countenance in this world to
> drown or hang themselves more than their even-Christen.
> (5.1.1–28)

Indeed, one cannot name a death suicide without establishing some agency of the victim, and one has to get rid of its traces to have the label withdrawn. The gravediggers' banter shows that the suicide verdict can be easily manipulated, also depending on linguistic choices. This in turn further inspires us to question the reliability of Gertrude's flowery account of Ophelia's death.

Another issue is raised here as well: the burial of a person who died by suicide. Back in the Renaissance, the coroner's juries were the ones to declare a death a suicide. There were many factors that could prevent them from giving an objective verdict (MacDonald and Murphy 1990, 22), bribery or social status of the deceased included, which is partly what the gravediggers allude to. Naming a death a suicide had repercussions, and those included the lack of proper Christian burial, often followed by popular punitive rituals desecrating the body (32). Ophelia, despite the nature of her death being obvious to the Gravedigger, receives a Christian burial due to her privileged background. However, it is emphasised repeatedly in the play that her treatment is exceptional, and that she in fact should not be having the burial rites she is having. Apart from the rustics' humorous conversation, some dissatisfaction is expressed by the Priest who has been called to administer Christian rites at her burial: to him, "She should in ground unsanctified been lodged / Till the last trumpet: for charitable prayers, / Flints and pebbles should be thrown on her" (5.1.14; 16–18).

All in all, there is a contrast between Gertrude and Laertes speaking of Ophelia's madness and death in highly poetic terms, not wanting to admit the ugly truth about her suffering and resolve to die, and people from the outside of the court, like the Gravedigger, his companion and the Priest, who reveal the repercussions the manner of her death poses, the shame and social ostracism which are written into it. Thus different perceptions of her death in the play balance one another out. Gertrude's idealised description of Ophelia's death is toned down by the rustics' mockery and the Priest's reluctance.

Hamlet is famously the character who talks about suicide most. In his first soliloquy he voices his disgust with the world's moral depravity, his mother being the prime example thereof, which inspires him to wish for death.

> O that this too too sallied flesh would melt,
> Thaw and resolve itself into a dew,
> Or that the Everlasting had not fixed

> His canon 'gainst self-slaughter. O God, God,
> How weary, stale, flat and unprofitable
> Seem to me all the uses of this world!
> Fie on't, ah, fie, 'tis an unweeded garden
> That grows to seed, things rank and gross in nature
> Possess it merely.
> (...)
> It is not, nor it cannot come to good;
> But break, my heart, for I must hold my tongue. (1.2.129–59)

He fantasises about the dissolution of his flesh, which would free him from the burden of life without any action on his part (1.2.129–30). Suicide is here a pleasurable fantasy, one to be pondered but not pursued, since it has been forbidden by God. Interesting here is the word "canon" (132) which, spoken, sounds the same as "cannon," suggesting an image of the warring godhead armed with a weapon to drive suicide away. "Break, my heart" (159) at the end can be interpreted both as a reminder that Hamlet has to endure his sorrow inwardly and not give anything away on the outside, and as another death wish, calling to his body to cease functioning. Hamlet's inclination towards suicide is thus curbed by the religious prohibition and converted into a more passive death wish, in tune with his general inertia throughout much of the play.

The second, and simultaneously the last instance where Hamlet explicitly considers suicide, is the famous "To be" monologue (3.1.55–87). While it has been argued that this speech could be about whether to take all sorts of action, as well as about specifically killing oneself (an argument that I find highly plausible is introduced by Fitzmaurice in "The corruption of Hamlet" (2010)), the suicide interpretation is the one most relevant to the topic of this chapter, and it is safe to assume that it is also the one most fixed in the critical and popular imagination alike.

The first half of the speech is organised through a juxtaposition of opposites in a neat syntactic pattern, each option being of roughly the same length so that the way the topic is tackled comes across as fair and unbiased, and true to the rules of rhetoric.

> To be, or not to be – that is the question;
> Whether 'tis nobler in the mind to suffer
> The slings and arrows of outrageous fortune
> Or to take arms against a sea of troubles
> And by opposing end them (...) (3.1.55–59)

The simple syntax of the first sentence lays down the dilemma – whether to kill oneself or not – with exceptional clarity. What immediately comes to mind is that it establishes suicide as a legitimate option. Living is no longer a given, it becomes a choice when one can also "not (...) be."

Suicide in juxtaposition with staying alive is here coming across as a more favourable option. Living is passively "suffering" (56), the alliteration and metre producing an emphasis on being in pain, through the "attack" of misfortunes. Conversely, taking one's own life is shown as the active solution of choosing to face and defeat the enemy.

> (...) to die: to sleep –
> No more, and by a sleep to say we end
> The heartache and the thousand natural shocks
> That flesh is heir to: 'tis a consummation
> Devoutly to be wished – to die: to sleep –
> To sleep, perchance to dream – ay, there's the rub,

> For in that sleep of death what dreams may come
> When we have shuffled off this mortal coil
> Must give us pause: there's the respect
> That makes calamity of so long life. (59–68)

The death – sleep conceit which follows offers an image that initially seems comforting and the subject matter seems to be judged favourably: death is presented as the end of worldly cares and perturbations of the flesh, and is "Devoutly to be wished" (63).

In the second part of the speech, however, we get a different perspective. Death is not just nothingness; there are "dreams," the afterlife, which has to be taken into the equation. The ensuing list of calamities that might befall one during life

> For who would bear the whips and scorns of time,
> Th'oppressor's wrong, the proud man's contumely,
> The pangs of despised love, the law's delay,
> The insolence of office and the spurns
> That patient merit of th'unworthy takes (...) (69–73)

lightens the tone and is puzzling, as it seems to mainly include annoying, but ultimately trivial matters that do not cause real suffering, the implication being that even those are enough to make one sick of living. In short, life brings so many misfortunes that anyone with any common sense would want to opt out. However, the fear of what could happen in the afterlife prevents most people from taking that step.

> When he himself might his quietus make
> With a bare bodkin. Who would fardels bear
> To grunt and sweat under a weary life

> But that the dread of something after death
> (The undiscovered country from whose bourn
> No traveller returns) puzzles the will
> And makes us rather bear those ills we have
> Than fly to others that we know not of.
> Thus conscience does make cowards –
> And thus the native hue of resolution
> Is sicklied o'er with the pale cast of thought,
> And enterprises of great pitch and moment
> With this regard their currents turn awry
> And lose the name of action. (74–87)

This consideration of life after death might be less relevant to the modern audience, among whom many might not believe in the afterlife at all. Therefore, it might not be as powerful and persuasive an argument against suicide as it was originally, especially since it is the only explicit argument against it.

I would, however, like to draw attention to the word "nobler" (56). It steers our attention towards Shakespeare's Roman plays, and it is not a coincidence that he was working on *Julius Caesar*, with its suicidal "noble Brutus," either right before or at the same time as he was writing *Hamlet*. Although the Roman notion of nobility seems to include suicide, in the monologue there is hinted a rivalling Christian paradigm, based on conscience[2] (Cantor 2004, 12). Within the framework of warfare, and the classical culture, where surrendering is a mark of dishonour, suicide is clearly suggested to be the elevated, "nobler" option. Nevertheless, conscience makes people "cowards" and

---

[2] For the explanation of why the standard sense of the word works better than "consciousness" see Wymer (1986, 31).

any resolve towards killing oneself is "sickled o'er" by "pale" thought. Shakespeare's other uses of the association of conscience with cowardice suggest that this type of cowardice is one we should succumb to rather than scorn, as it prevents one from making morally wrong choices (Wymer 1986, 32).

Aside from those few instances where suicide is an overt topic of discussion, Hamlet consistently shows a profound disregard for his life (and sometimes even afterlife) throughout the play. Preparing for the first encounter with the Ghost, given that it does indeed resemble his father, he resolves to "speak to it, though hell itself should gape" (1.2.243). When Horatio advises him not to follow the Ghost, his answer is: "I do not set my life at a pin's fee, / And for my soul – what can it do to that, / Being a thing immortal as itself?" (1.4.75–77) and Horatio's implicit suggestion that the Ghost might tempt his friend into suicide (79–88) is completely ignored by him. When "mad" Hamlet's riddled speech wearies Polonius and the latter announces that he is going to "take leave," the former offers him some reassurance, saying: "You cannot take from me anything that I will not more willingly part withal – except my life, except my life, except my life" (2.2.210–12). Then, even though ultimately he manages to avoid being executed on Claudius' orders, Hamlet does nothing to avoid being sent away to England in the first place, even though he suspects his uncle of bad intentions, and he seems to have escaped largely by chance. Having run away, he decides to go back to the court where he will be at the mercy of the very person who tried to have him killed.

Finally, when challenged to a duel which will ultimately prove fatal to him, Hamlet admits a feeling of misgiving to Horatio, and then disregards it: "Thou wouldst not think how ill all's here about my heart – but it is no matter" (5.2.190–91). When Horatio tells him that in such a case he probably should not fight, he is adamant about doing it regardless, asserting a "special providence in the fall of a sparrow" and that "[t]he readiness is all, since no man of aught he leaves knows what is't to leave betimes" (5.2.197–201). Here Hamlet's assertion that one should avoid thinking about a potential outcome, and instead accept and face whatever comes, including untimely death, does provides a possible explanation for his participation in the duel. On the other hand, it seems discordant with his earlier anger at his mother and uncle, and the promise of revenge to the Ghost, and rules out the reading of his earlier decisions as consistent surrendering to Providence. Hamlet's expressions of either indifference towards or yearning for potential death, together with his disregard of and even occasionally running into situations that are likely to be deadly for him, can be read as suicidal in itself, even though he does not literally commit suicide. It has to be acknowledged, though, that Hamlet's death in the final duel, especially considering his decision to fight Laertes despite the "ill-feeling," is very much open to a stage interpretation as a veiled suicide, although I think of it more as a resignation.

What to make of the non-suicidal death of a character who contemplated suicide? I propose that it can be read as a partial fulfilment of Hamlet's death-wish from his first soliloquy where he fantasised about dying yet wanted it to happen without having to kill himself for fear of damnation. Thus, he manages to both have his proverbial cake and eat it. Moreover, he is forgiven for his wrongdoings by Laertes and his narrative of the events at Elsinore will spread through Horatio. This is a rather favourable outcome for the Prince. It is, however, an ambiguous ending for the kingdom: the queen, the king and his immediate heir dead, the crown to be claimed by an impulsive and war-loving individual, hurriedly named the new heir for lack of better alternatives.

The duel inspires new suicidal impulses. Seeing that his friend is about to die, Horatio immediately wants to kill himself, stating that he is "more an antique Roman than a Dane" (5.2.325). Even though he tries to frame this attempt as a noble Roman suicide, one cannot help but notice that acting on impulse is very out of character for Horatio, who is one of the most prudent characters in the play, and whom Hamlet admires for not letting emotions get the better of him.

A highly unresolved moment, and one often unremarked by critics, is Gertrude's drinking from the poisoned cup. I will not attempt to prove the precise nature of her death; nonetheless, it is worth briefly considering the implications of reading this as a suicide. Shakespeare's Gertrude is enigmatic and underwritten, and so putting her among Shakespeare's only three onstage female suicides: Juliet, Cleopatra and her maid Charmian, gives a new perspective on her character. The first two, in contrast to Gertrude, are eponymous heroines of their plays, the third is a loyal servant and confidante to one of them. From Cleopatra's staged suicide, matched by an ecstatic speech, to Juliet's succinct, but adequate words, to Charmian's open defiance of the Romans, Gertrude's last words, "The drink, the drink – I am poisoned" (5.2.295) sound rather underwhelming. Moreover, it can be concluded from her son's words "I dare not drink yet, madam" (276) that Gertrude offers a cup to Hamlet. That poses a question that the text leaves open: is it the same cup she has just drunk from? A performance that chooses such an interpretation has to deal with its heavy implications: Gertrude only tells her son that her own cup is poisoned much later (294–295), which would mean she literally wants to murder him at this point. Why would she want that? Regardless of the degree of her possible complicity in Old Hamlet's death, she is shown throughout to care about her son to some extent, and so this appears out of character. It could, however, be read as a double defiance of Claudius' orders: she drinks poison herself, refusing to continue being accessory to his scheming. Yet in being the one to poison Hamlet, she removes the satisfaction of doing so from the King; drinking from the same cup as Hamlet is a morbid reaffirmation of their familial bond. This fails, and Gertrude's dying words firmly place the blame on Claudius, exposing his crime, while at the same time positioning her as a victim.

Conclusion

Both *Hamlet* and *Romeo and Juliet* have moments when suicide is brought to the fore for audiences and readers to view, examine and judge. As in most of Shakespeare's plays, different viewpoints on the given issue are scattered throughout the text, inviting the reader/spectator to pick them up and make sense of them. On the level of a single phrase, sentence or speech, one is likely to find, among others, few passages where suicide seems to be elevated: painted either as a valid solution to problems encountered by characters, a much needed instrument of restoring some of the seemingly lost agency, and sometimes even a pretty way to die. Taken out of context, those can have a damaging impact on vulnerable audiences.

Nonetheless, those moments and scenes cannot be viewed in detachment from the big picture, the internal logic of a play, and their relation with other means of signification present in it. And it is in the process of integrating those instances into the larger network of meanings that their own relevance changes and gives way to a more balanced view of suicide in the plays. Ophelia's suicide might be pretty when reported, but when considered together with the rustics' down-to-earth practical and literal attitude, it becomes a complex event, one that cannot be detached from its sociocultural and legal ramifications. Romeo and Juliet might be made into statues, but is this newly attained longevity true or illusory, and, even more importantly, is it what the lovers actually wanted?

Does that mean we should not be concerned about the depiction of suicide in those plays at all? The answer is: not entirely. The tendency to take Shakespeare out of context is rife, especially on the web. In fact, it has always been present to some extent, starting with quotations put down by the original audiences in the commonplace books. Better reading comprehension might be taught and good practices for understanding Shakespeare can be encouraged, but ultimately this tendency is something that cannot be changed in its entirety. We also need to take account of the long tradition of romanticising Ophelia's distraught and/or dead image, inspired by Romantics and brought to its peak by John Everett Millais's famous Pre-Raphaelite painting. It is a tradition that it will take a long time to undo.

From yet another perspective, this chapter has been a mainly textual consideration of the representation of a delicate theme which might be treated quite differently in performance. A director might choose to highlight those tiny moments where suicide is presented favourably and brush over those that point to the devastation it can wreak. Therefore, each performance needs to be assessed individually, and the audiences need to be appropriately informed before seeing ones that might be harmful to those more vulnerable.

References

Ayers, John W. et al. 2017. "Internet Searches for Suicide Following the Release of *13 Reasons Why*." *JAMA Internal Medicine* 177(10), 1528–1529.

Burton, Robert. 2022. *The Anatomy of Melancholy*. Vol. I. Oxford Scholarly Editions Online. Eds. Thomas C. Faulkner et al. Oxford University Press.

https://www.oxfordscholarlyeditions.com/display/10.1093/actrade/ 9780198124481.book.1/actrade-9780198124481-book-1?rskey=dxAr- H7&result=3 (accessed 14 July 2023).

Campbell, Denis. 2017. "Netflix Show Condemned for 'Romanticising' Teenager's Suicide." https://www.theguardian.com/media/2017/apr/21/netflix-13-reasons-why-condemned-for-romanticising-suicide (accessed 14 July 2023).

Cantor, Paul A. 2004. *Hamlet and the Renaissance.* Cambridge. Cambridge University Press.

Crawford, Nicholas. 2015. "We'll Always Have Paris: The Third Household and the 'Bed of Death' in *Romeo and Juliet.*" *Shakespeare Survey* 68, 323–336.

Cribb, T. J. 1982. "The Unity of *Romeo and Juliet.*" *Shakespeare Survey* 34, 93–104.

Centers for Disease Control and Prevention. 2023. "WISQARS. Leading Causes of Death Visualisation Tool." https://wisqars.cdc.gov/data/lcd/home (accessed 14 July 2023).

Dessen, Alan C. 1995. "Romeo Opens the Tomb." In: Alan C. Dessen, *Recovering Shakespeare's Theatrical Vocabulary.* Cambridge. Cambridge University Press, 176–195.

Drew, Daniel. 2022. *Joy of the Worm: Suicide and Pleasure in Early Modern English Literature.* Chicago. University of Chicago Press.Fernie, Ewan. 2017. *Shakespeare for Freedom: Why Plays Matter.* Cambridge. Cambridge University Press.

Fitzmaurice, Andrew. 2010. "The corruption of Hamlet." In: *Shakespeare and Early Modern Political Thought.* Eds. David Armitage, Conal Condren and Andrew Fitzmaurice. Cambridge. Cambridge University Press, 139–56.

Gouge, William. 1637. "Preface." In: John Sym, *Lives Preservative against Self-killing. Or, An Usefull Treatise Concerning Life and Self-Murder Shewing the Kindes, and Meanes of Them Both: The Excellency and Preservation of the Former: The Evill, and Prevention of the Latter. Containing the Resolution of Manifold Cases, and Questions Concerning That Subject; with Plentifull Variety of Necessary and Usefull Observations, and Practical Directions, Needfull for All Christians.* https://www.proquest.com/docview/2240893500/99853281 (accessed 14 July 2023).

Grady, Hugh. 2009. *Shakespeare and Impure Aesthetics.* Cambridge. Cambridge University Press.

Henick, Mark. 2017. "Why *13 Reasons Why* Is Dangerous." https://edition.cnn.com/2017/05/03/opinions/13-reasons-why-gets-it-wrong-henick-opinion/index.html (accessed 24 February 2023).

Kahn, Coppélia. 1977. "Coming of Age in Verona." *Modern Language Studies* 8(1), 5–22.

Kleiner, John. 2014. "Live Boys—Dead Girls: Death and False Death in *Romeo and Juliet*." *Literary Imagination* 17(1), 18–34.

Kottman, Paul A. 2012. "Defying the Stars: Tragic Love as the Struggle for Freedom in *Romeo and Juliet*." *Shakespeare Quarterly* 63(1), 1–38.

Kristeva, Julia. 1987. "Romeo and Juliet: Love-Hatred in the Couple." In: *Tales of Love.* Translated by Leon S. Roudiez. New York. Columbia University Press, 209–233.

Langley, Eric. 2009. *Narcissism and Suicide in Shakespeare and His Contemporaries.* Oxford. Oxford University Press.

Levenson, Jill L. 1996. "Shakespeare's *Romeo and Juliet*: The Places of Invention." *Shakespeare Survey* 49, 45–56.

—. 2000. "Echoes Inhabit a Garden: The Narratives of *Romeo and Juliet*." *Shakespeare Survey* 53, 39–48.

MacDonald, Michael 1986. "Ophelia's Maimed Rites." *Shakespeare Quarterly* 37(3), 309–317.

MacDonald, Michael and Terence R. Murphy. 1990. *Sleepless Souls: Suicide in Early Modern England.* Oxford. Oxford University Press.

Macfie, Pamela Royston. 2022. "'Native and Indued / Unto that Element': Dissolution, Permeability, and the Death of Ophelia." In: *Shakespearean Death Arts: Hamlet Among the Tombs.* Eds. William E. Engel and Grant Williams. Zurich. Palgrave Macmillan, 241–260.

McLuskie, Kathleen E. 1971. "Shakespeare's 'Earth-Treading Stars:' The Image of the Masque in *Romeo and Juliet*." *Shakespeare Survey* 24, 63–70.

Mendoza, Kirsten. 2019. "Sexual Violence, Trigger Warnings and the Early Modern Classroom." In: *Teaching Social Justice Through Shakespeare: Why Renaissance*

Literature Matters Now. Eds. Hillary Eklund and Wendy Beth Hyman. Edinburgh. Edinburgh University Press, 97–105.

Niederkrotenthaler, Thomas et al. 2019. "Association of Increased Youth Suicides in the United States With the Release of *13 Reasons Why*." *JAMA Psychiatry* 76(9), 933–940.

O'Neill, Stephen. 2014. *Shakespeare and YouTube: New Media Forms of the Bard*. London. Bloomsbury Publishing Plc.

Oxford University Press. 2022. "romanticize" (v). Oxford English Dictionary Online. https://www.oed.com/view/Entry/167132?redirectedFrom=romanticise& (accessed 3 February 2023).

Reddit. 2023. "Stop Romanticizing Suicide." https://www.reddit.com/r/teenagers/comments/10toed6/stop_romanticizing_suicide/ (accessed 22 February 2023).

Shakespeare, William. 2016. *Hamlet*. Eds. Ann Thompson and Neil Taylor. London. Bloomsbury Arden Shakespeare.

—. 1623. *Mr. William Shakespeares Comedies, Histories, & Tragedies. Published according to the true originall copies*. https://www.proquest.com/docview/2240890297/99846615 (accessed 27 March 2023).

—. 2012. *Romeo and Juliet*. Ed. René Weis. London. Bloomsbury Arden Shakespeare.

Snyder, Susan. 1995. "Ideology and the Feud in *Romeo and Juliet*." *Shakespeare Survey* 49, 87–96.

Tronicke, Marlena. 2018. *Shakespeare's Suicides: Dead Bodies That Matter*. New York. Routledge.

Williams, Zoe. 2017. "Netflix's *13 Reasons Why* and the Trouble with Dramatizing Suicide." https://www.theguardian.com/tv-and-radio/2017/apr/26/netflix-13-reasons-why-suicide (accessed 24 February 2023).

World Health Organization. 2021. "Suicide: Key Facts." https://www.who.int/newsroom/fact-sheets/detail/suicide (accessed 21 February 2023).

Wymer, Rowland. 1986. *Suicide and Despair in the Jacobean Drama*. Brighton. The Harvester Press.

AGNIESZKA ROMANOWSKA

4.
Hag-Seed by Margaret Atwood as a Meta-artistic Exploration of William Shakespeare's *The Tempest*

Introduction

The Tempest, "this haunting, conflicted, and mysterious play" (Dobson and Wells 2001, 473), has a long and rich history of adaptations, appropriations and rewritings. What attracts adaptors and provokes reinterpretations is its openness and ambiguity manifested in the relatively loose plot, unspecified setting, variety of form and tone, and the indefinite ending that leaves the reader or viewer with more questions than answers. Moreover, the play's "rich allusiveness opens up multiple perspectives that resist easy synthesis" (Lindley 2002, 81). W.H. Auden connects the play's adaptive flexibility to its mythopoeic qualities. *The Sea and the Mirror*, his poetic "Commentary on Shakespeare's *The*

Tempest," testifies to the correctness of Auden's claim that *The Tempest* inspires people "to go on for themselves" (Auden 2002, 297) and devise their own versions of Shakespeare's characters and their own revisions of his plots.

It has to be admitted that attempts to modify a literary work so that it fits new tastes and conventions may, sometimes, prove fatal to its original substance. Such was the case at the early stages of the play's reception when, in 1667, John Dryden and William Davenant reshaped it into a Restoration comedy, *The Tempest, or The Enchanted Island*, and Thomas Shadwell embellished it with operatic elements some years later. These rewritings proved so popular and influential that they virtually displaced the source text, so that for the next century and a half "most English readers and audiences apparently assumed that the Dryden-Davenant-Shadwell versions were identical to Shakespeare's drama" (Vaughan and Vaughan 1999, 76), and it was not until the beginning of Romanticism that their "frippery and licentiousness fell out of favour" (Voigts 2014, 44). But, most frequently, with Shakespeare being, apparently, "infinitely interpretable" (Atwood 2016a), the adaptive creativity is a blessing rather than a curse, resulting in revisitations that imaginatively interact with his plays. More often than not, the revisions capitalise on the canonical position and rich cultural legacy of Shakespeare's texts, while, at the same time, in their dialogic – sometimes polemic – character, they reflect the changing socio-historical, and critical, paradigms.

In one of the chapters of *The Cambridge Companion to Shakespeare's Last Plays*, Virginia Mason Vaughan analyses several literary invocations of *The Tempest* to identify the ways in which their authors respond to the play's focus on the role, function and limitations of art in human life. While the questions about the consoling, restorative and transformational powers of art, artistic creation and artistic illusion belong to the leading concerns in Shakespeare's *oeuvre* in general, his conclusions are not unambiguous, the least so in *The Tempest*. Prospero pays a high price for his detachment from the material reality of governing, but the powers that he still possesses allow him to survive and control the environment of the island and its inhabitants. The last manifestations of his art – the storm devised to affect the consciences of his adversaries and the wedding masque to celebrate the betrothal of Miranda and Ferdinand – leave him only partly successful, as regards the first undertaking, and irritated, as regards the second. Caliban's persistent enmity and Antonio's silence in the scene of reconciliation may be seen as undermining, or at least questioning, the healing powers of his endeavours. The finale is open-ended: Prospero breaks his staff and asks to be released from the confines of his own creation, while his future as the restored ruler of Milan is obscure. It is perhaps precisely because the play "remains elusive about the role of art" (Vaughan 2009, 156) that it has always provoked writers to inspect this issue in their own versions. Vaughan discusses a number of rewritings and literary responses to the play, as different as Robert Browning's dramatic monologue, "Caliban upon Setebos," Percy MacKaye's masque, *Caliban by the Yellow Sands*, Auden's poetic triptych, *The Sea and the Mirror*, Hilda Doolittle's *By Avon River*, and the novels *The Diviners* by Margaret Laurence, *Indigo* by Marina Warner, and *Mama Day* by Gloria Naylor. Although these authors represent a variety of perspectives on the issue of art *versus* reality, they all – Vaughan concludes – share the conviction that the "committed writer must never give up magic, no matter how painful it may be" (2009, 170). The most decisive test of the value and power of art, she claims, are the audience's reactions and what stays with them after the reading experience. "Perhaps that is the ultimate answer to questions about the efficacy of art. For the poets, playwrights and novelists (...), the literary work matters insofar as it works on the mind and heart of its intended audience" (Vaughan 2009, 171).

In this chapter, Margaret Atwood's novel, *Hag-Seed* (2016b), will be discussed as yet another instance of a literary response to Shakespeare's romance which focuses on the issues of art and artistic creation. The first section of the chapter discusses the publishing project that initiated Atwood's novel. "Going on for [herself]," Atwood engages in an imaginative and multifaceted dialogue with *The Tempest*, a dialogue which she develops into a dense and intricate web of meta-artistic interactions. These are analysed in the main section of the chapter. In its final section it is argued that part of the criticism this otherwise generally well-received novel evoked, can be explained by the commentators' overlooking, or ignoring, what seems to have been Atwood's main interest: to play a kind of literary game with Shakespeare[1] – writer against writer. A game that engages the participants in ruminations about the meaning of art, the significance and potential of artistic creation and the responsibilities of an artist.

Hogarth Shakespeare and its literary game

An instructive starting point for the discussion of *Hag-Seed* as a meta-artistic literary game is to inspect the origin of this adaptation.

---

[1] The phrase "playing games with Shakespeare," as an image referring to the process of reception, was coined by the organizers of the 2. International Shakespeare Conference held in 2004 in Gdańsk. I find this metaphor very apt because it not only testifies to the existence of the "living record" Shakespeare hoped for, but also expresses the creativity and imaginativeness necessary in any interaction with a canonical work of art that has an ambition of being something more than a crude modernisation. See the volume edited by Olga Kubińska and Ewa Nawrocka, *Playing Games with Shakespeare. Contemporary Reception of Shakespeare in the Baltic Region*, Gdańsk 2004.

Atwood's novel was published as one of the titles issued in the Hogarth Shakespeare Series,[2] an initiative launched by the established London publisher, Hogarth Press, imprint of Penguin Random House, in connection with the worldwide celebrations of two milestone Shakespearean anniversaries, the 450th anniversary of his birth in 2014 and the quatercentenary of his death in 2016. In the Hogarth Shakespeare Project, eight well-known contemporary novelists were commissioned to produce prose retellings of the plays they chose. Hogarth Books, originally founded by Leonard and Virginia Woolf, has always strived to publish significant writers and notable titles, and is nowadays advertised as "an adventurous fiction imprint with an accent on the pleasures of storytelling and a broad awareness of the world," "taking inspiration form the past" (Hogarth). Created under the auspices of the Hogarth project, Atwood's novel represents the publisher's "coherent programme to update Shakespeare in 'literary retellings' (…) different from the idiosyncratic one-off adaptations that have tended to characterise novelisations to this point" (Lanier 2017, 231). In his discussion of the Hogarth series, Lanier identifies various ways in which Shakespeare's iconic literariness was reconfigured to accommodate the change of mode, and the loss of language, in the context of the publisher's ambition to offer high-quality literary retellings. Indeed, at the core of the undertaking which resulted in Atwood's contribution is a literary encounter between a canonical author of an impact that surpasses the canon, one who, in Harold Bloom's famous

---

[2]   Ultimately, the series consists of seven novels (the re-telling of *Hamlet*, initially planned to be released in 2021, has never materialized): Jeanette Winterson, *The Gap of Time* based on *The Winter's Tale* (2015); Margaret Atwood's *Hag-Seed* on *The Tempest* (2016); Howard Jacobson's *Shylock Is My Name* on *The Merchant of Venice* (2016); Anne Tyler's *Vinegar Girl* on *The Taming of the Shrew* (2016); Edward St. Aubyn's *Dunbar* on *King Lear* (2017); Tracy Chevalier's *New Boy* on *Othello* (2017) and Jo Nesbo's *Macbeth* on *Macbeth* (2018).

formulation, "invented us, and continues to contain us" (1997, xvi) and "writers that you already know and love" (Hogarth).

From the way the series was advertised in a short video in which the authors talk about their reactions to the invitation and about their objectives, it is clear that Hogarth Press counted on the incentive provided by three factors: "The world's favourite playwright," "Today's best-loved novelists" and "Timeless stories retold."[3] These slogans demonstrate what Linda Hutcheon describes as the natural joys of adaptation. Humans enjoy variations on what they already know and therefore they enjoy adaptation, a culturally creative interaction which offers "repetition but without replication, bringing together the comfort of ritual and recognition with the delight of surprise and novelty. (…) it involves both memory and change, persistence and variation" (Hutcheon 2006, 173). Yet, in a project highlighting its concern with literariness, it was apparently felt that rewriting Shakespeare's language into modern prose needed some justification, so the video ends with the closing words of sonnet 18 – "So long as men can breathe or eyes can see, / So long lives this, and this gives life to thee." This was done, on the one hand, to underscore the homage-paying character of the venture that honours Shakespeare's unprecedented cultural legacy, and, on the other, "to negotiate (…) the gap between the literary, with its connotations of continuity and quality, and popular adaptation, with its association with generic templates and ephemeral mass appeal" (Lanier 2017, 232). Nowadays, in an age "conductive to sampling and appropriation as creative activities, adaptation has become more widely perceived as genuinely artistic and thus potentially compatible with literariness" (Lanier 2017, 237). As a result, such projects as the Hogarth Shakespeare can be conceived with a comfortable awareness

---

[3] https://www.youtube.com/watch?v=ERpZTHYB3kA (accessed 15 July 2023).

that the rewritings will be received as self-standing creations, "ones that provide new cultural content in an increasingly diverse range of contexts and communities. (...) influential and agenda-setting in their own right" (Sanders 2006, 212). Taking all this into consideration, it can be assumed that the novelists participating in the project worked with the reassuring feeling that their contributions were perceived as independent artistic undertakings, allowing for a considerable creative freedom. Even if "with all the rewrites of Shakespeare and Austen routinely thrown at readers nowadays" (Groskop 2016), there was some risk of a lukewarm, if not utterly distanced, readers' response.

Because the main idea behind the project was to produce novelistic versions of the plays that modernised Shakespeare's dramas in a way that nevertheless would allow readers to recognise the source texts, the publishers were cautious enough to use the label "retellings" to describe the products of their venture. Reviewers and critics followed, using a plethora of other, more or less metaphorical, descriptions – rewriting, revisiting, refashioning, reimagining. In an attempt to categorise Atwood's contribution in the more formal terms of adaptation and appropriation, Sofía Muñoz-Valdivieso – referring to Julie Sanders's concepts of closeness and distance in relation to the source text – concludes that "matters are far from clear-cut, since the resonances of *The Tempest* in the novel are at the same time obvious and discreet, blatant and nearly invisible" (2017, 109). On the one hand, she claims, the novelist dutifully realises the publisher's agenda in paying tribute to Shakespeare and celebrating the cultural capital his work constitutes. Yet, on the other hand, "Atwood the magician cannot resist the challenge to seize *The Tempest* and make it her own – or (...) collaborate with Shakespeare to make something of their own" (109).[4]

---

[4] Dana Percec has argued persuasively that Atwood diverges from the contemporary interpretations of the play, as well as her own preferences as a novelist, and "gives up her usual dystopias for a less predictable scenario" (Percec 2018, 295).

The idea of playing a game with Shakespeare, which was part and parcel of the Hogarth Press undertaking, must have appeared the more exciting to Atwood because it was to be performed in a way more explicit than by means of allusions and references, as she had done many times before.

While rewriting was a common procedure in Shakespeare's day – the playwright himself being credited with his own plots in just two cases out of the thirty-eight plays that constitute his canon – "today's inclusive, global, intertextual awareness has made the reading of one text against another compulsory, and thus the pressure for 'originality' more dramatic" (Percec 2018, 296). The Hogarth Press took pains to underscore that, although the series is meant to bring Shakespeare closer to contemporary readers in a form more accessible than that of a play-text, the involved authors were to use the plays "to create something entirely their own."[5] In view of what has been said about the meta-artistic character of the engagement that the project allowed, Atwood's choice of *The Tempest* – a play which "constitutes a complete contextualisation of metatheatrical elements in the way it is replete with audiences, masques, and explicit allusions to the world of theatre" (Tatar 2020, 95) – does not come as surprising. Since Atwood first encountered Shakespeare in high school, he has been one of the most important influences on her own writing, and his last romance, which has always been her favourite play precisely because of its meta-theatricality, she finds "especially intriguing because of the many questions it leaves unanswered" (blurb). Some of these questions that must have occurred to Atwood as vital are linked to her own concerns, as poet and novelist, about the convergence of art and power, or rather – about the artist's position as an illusionist and manipulator, and the social responsibility that ensues

---

[5] https://www.youtube.com/watch?v=ERpZTHYB3kA (accessed 15 July 2023).

from it. As she voices it in her book *Negotiating with the Dead: A Writer on Writing*, "Prospero uses his arts – magic arts, arts of illusion – not just for entertainment, though he does some of that as well, but for the purposes of moral and social improvement. That being said, it must also be said that Prospero plays God" (Atwood 2002, 115).[6]

Although the novel is intriguingly multilayered and, like *The Tempest*, invites a variety of interpretations, the basic storyline of *Hag-Seed* is easy to summarise. The main protagonist, Felix Phillips, is a successful theatre director ousted from his position as Artistic Director at the Makeshiweg Theatre Festival by his friend and assistant, Anthony Price. While Felix was increasingly preoccupied with his inventive, and controversial, stagings of Shakespeare's plays, Tony was gradually taking over his administrative and financial duties and gathering supporters in the festival's board to get rid of him. Felix, furious when informed about the termination of his contract and the cancellation of his newest production of *The Tempest*, is devastated on a more personal level, too. *The Tempest*, more experimental than anything he had created before, in which he was planning to play the role of Prospero, was a form of healing from his prolonged mourning after the death of his daughter, Miranda. Orphaned by her mother at childbirth, the girl died at the age of three as Felix, busy with the festival, overlooked early symptoms of meningitis – or so he now claims, struggling with feelings of guilt and sorrow. Felix, overwhelmed by this double loss, retires to a secluded dilapidated woodland cottage and begins plotting revenge against Tony while living at the verge of reality and hallucinations, engrossed in his imagined family life, with the ghost Miranda growing up and accompanying him in this social

---

[6] On Atwood's use of the narrative strategy of "godgame," see Kuester 2019.

and emotional exile. After nine years of such a life, increasingly aware that he is heading towards insanity, Felix, under the false name of Mr Duke, undertakes a job as a literature teacher in Fletcher County Correctional Institute, a nearby penitentiary institution, and comes back to Shakespeare's plays which he successfully stages together with his inmates/students. As his prison classes and performances draw the attention of government officials, a ministerial delegation is planning to visit the institution to watch the play and decide about the future of the literacy programme. A prospect of revenge appears when Felix learns that the delegation will include the very same people who years ago dismissed him from his post, now important figures in the Canadian government. Felix decides to revive his long-lost project on *The Tempest* and – with the help of digital media, blackmail, drugs and his dedicated actors – in an impressive, if hardly credible, theatrical *coup de force* manages to make his adversaries confess their past dishonest actions, install him back in his former position as the head of the festival and secure the financial future of the Fletcher Correctional theatre.

Even from this general summary of the plot it is evident that Atwood never loses sight of what evidently is the core of her approach – she reads *The Tempest* "as a metatheatrical text about an aged director who seems to believe in the nobleness of his enterprise as a means to an end, but also as an engrossing project in and of itself" (Muñoz-Valdivieso 2017, 110). I would argue that Atwood's endeavour is both metatheatrical and metaliterary and, therefore, in what follows, I am using a more general term which encompasses these two elements – meta-artistic.[7]

---

[7] For a concise discussion of the theory of metatextuality in literature and theatre, see: Tatar 2020, 93–95.

"My high charms work" – levels of interaction

The meta-artistic interactions of Atwood's novel with its hypotext[8] are numerous and can be traced on many different levels, from wordplays on the characters' names to the creative modulation of the play's central thematic concerns. *The Tempest*'s story is reshaped along multiple paths of Atwood's plot, whose frame, like that of its Renaissance source, is circular: Felix's downfall is associated with his preparations to stage *The Tempest* with himself in the leading role, the period of his seclusion in the country shade is marked by his relationship with the imaginary daughter – thus being a version of Prospero and Miranda's exile, and his revengeful revival is connected to the new production of the same play. Circularity is visible also on the level of imagery and symbolism. The novel begins with a theatrical storm in the screening of the opening scene from *The Tempest*'s production by Felix and his Fletcher Correctional Players. The tempest is verbally created by the Announcer in his first rap piece: "What you're gonna see, is a storm at sea: / Winds are howlin', sailors yowlin', / Passengers cursin' 'em" (3),[9] then visualised by the "screengrab from the Tornado Channel. Stock shot of ocean waves. Stock shot of rain" (4) and by the camera zooming in "on a bathtub-toy sailboat tossing up and down on a blue plastic shower curtain with fish on it, the waves made by hands underneath" (4). In the epilogue of the novel, Felix and Estelle are leaving for a cruise to the

---

[8] In Gérard Genette's categorization of various palimpsestic interactions between literary texts, the hypotext is the earlier text that the hypertext derives from (Genette 1997, 7).

[9] In this chapter, wherever the novel is quoted, the numbers in brackets refer to page numbers in the following edition: Atwood 2016b.

Caribbean, taking with them 8Handz, the Ariel actor, who, having been granted early parole, "deserved a break, considering all the hard work he'd done for Felix. (...) and the sea air would be so liberating for him" (282–283). From the vulnerable vessel tossed by the waves of the cleansing deluge of the storm to the regenerating peacefulness of the calm sea and the reassuring safety of a gigantic holiday cruise ship – in this way, imagery connected with water, sea and sea voyage is, as in the play, consistently employed to depict the characters' transformations.

The transformational aspects of Atwood's retelling are also visible in the symbolic quality of the time frame. The twelve years of Prospero's stay on the island get reinvented into the time span of Felix's exile in the woodland hut, from the moment he loses his daughter and his post as the artistic director of the festival to the day he gets employed as teacher in the Literacy Through Literature high school level programme at the Fletcher County Correctional Institute. This moment signals the beginning of a slow process of regeneration after having spent too much time "alone with his grief eating away at him, too much time gnawing on his grievances. He felt as if he were waking up from a long and melancholy dream" (48). But Felix's psychological prison time is much longer: it is at the beginning of the fourth year of his job in prison that Estelle, his "auspicious star," announces the ministerial visit and Felix realises that an opportunity for revenge has appeared. His prison Tempest is prepared within the symbolic time span of the three months between January 7 and March 31. From the wintertime exhaustion caused by shovelling "his car out from the windrow thrown by the snowplough across the top of his laneway" (67) to the hopeful spring with the prospect of the tropical vacation on the Caribbean that "would be lovely at this time of year" (282). Also, Atwood carefully constructs the opening retrospections to illustrate the extent to which Felix lives on and in his recollections. The temporal plane is for her as flexible as it is for Shakespeare, who thematises the issue of memory and recollection by introducing the reported past into his play, and thus complicating the apparent adherence to the unity of time. Can we actually talk about unity of time, if so much depends on Prospero's reporting at length the events from twelve years ago and on Ariel's and Caliban's awareness-shaping recollections of the time before their servitude?[10]

One level of Atwood's meta-artistic game is visible already in the table of contents. The novel mimics the play in the division of its content into five sections ("acts"), each containing eight to ten chapters ("scenes"), preceded by a prologue and closing with an epilogue. Additionally, some of the chapters feature "stage directions," like "Monday, January 7, 2013" or "The same day." In this way, Atwood signals the formal complexity that results from her deliberate and intricate blending of Shakespeare's play and her own text. The adapting novelist enhances the level of meta-literary and meta-theatrical game by making the staging of the play on which the novel is based the central element of her retelling. As Shakespeare's play-within-a-play – the masque – gets abruptly interrupted by Prospero, so the staging of the play-within-a-novel is only fragmentary, turning into riot and kidnapping.[11] This is necessary for the development of the plot. But the essence of Atwood's meta-artistic endeavour is the task of turning the play-text – a script for performance to be watched – into the text of a novel in which any spectacle has to be imagined

---

[10] Cf. Vaughan and Vaughan 1999, 15.

[11] This is an example of numerous analogies created by Atwood, who relies on the "mirror technique, juxtaposing elements from Shakespeare's original play with a modern plotline that reflects them " (Lanier 2017, 242).

by individual readers, not enacted in front of their eyes. Her material is text on page, and her matter is literary. Unlike a playwright, she does not use language to encode any potential theatrical realization, but to contemplate the art of theatre and its possible transformational qualities via the act of writing a novelistic retelling of a drama. Not quite aware that he is being transformed himself, Felix witnesses many times the emotions of his actors as they watch the video recordings of their productions, complete with the credits. "Everyone in the class – even the bit parts, even the understudies – got to see his stage name in lights. (...) Watching the many faces watching their own faces as they pretended to be someone else – Felix found that strangely moving. For once in their lives, they loved themselves" (58).

Atwood focuses at length on the process of creating Felix's prison production of *The Tempest*, reporting on the preparations in detail – his classroom analysis of the play-text, interpretation of the characters, listing the play's key concerns; his casting decisions; preparation of the costumes and properties, the rehearsals and, finally, the video recording of the scenes that must, for security reasons, substitute any live performance before the prison audience. To the most challenging aspects of the production belong the characters of Miranda and Ariel, especially the latter's fairy nature and magical powers. The first problem is solved by bringing in a real actress. The second one requires a persuasive interpretation which Felix, as an experienced director, quite easily supplies. After having learned that Ariel is "the special-effects guy (...) like a digital expert. He's doing 3-D virtual reality. (...) Lighting, sound, computer simulation" (104), all of the initially unwilling inmates want to take this role. Atwood's novelistic instincts suggested substituting Prospero's art with the "magic" of modern technology: superpowers turn into electronic devices and technology-created illusion. The third major challenge concerns Shakespeare's, and Atwood's, basic tool – language. The inmates find the exposition too long. "Plus it's boring. Even Miranda finds it boring. She almost goes to sleep," SnakeEye complains to Felix. So when his team offers instead a rap-opera summary of act 1 scene 2, Felix has to give in – although he feels deprived of his scene – because "isn't this what he's asked them to do? Rethink, reframe?" (155). When a few days later the actors devise a special self-introductory piece for Caliban, he has to admit that, although they are "crapping up [his] play" (176), "[he] did encourage them to write their own extra material, so he's not entitled to be grumpy" (173). The fact that Atwood introduces the theme of adapting Shakespeare for the stage is another meta-artistic gesture of hers. It exposes her own role as an adapting novelist, at the same time allowing her to comment on various forms of adaptation, its reasons and objectives. In creating the lyrics for the rapping actors, Atwood is inventive, exploratory and never plays a false tone. She provides evidence that an adaptation makes sense if it opens new vistas for exploration and if it resonates with the recipients.

Quite expectedly in a novel that is an ambitious literary game played with Shakespeare, language is in the centre of attention. The simplest manifestation of Atwood's creative approach to language is the wordplay involving the characters' names. The telling name of Prospero becomes substituted with a semantically close counterpart, Felix. Anthony Price stands for Prospero's brother, Antonio. Felix's second adversary, Sal, is given a name which is a blend of Antonio's ally, Alonso, and his brother, Sebastian. Sal's son Freddie is a clear allusion to Ferdinand. In most cases these name-plays depend on the phonetic and visual qualities of the words, which is evident in the case of Miranda and the actress hired to play her, Anne-Marie. Hag-Seed, the name for Caliban, is a special case because it is both a quotation and a curse. While in inventing the main characters' names, Atwood made it easy for readers to recognise their Shakespearean prototypes and thus exposed the links with her source text, in the case of the inmates' names she granted herself unrestricted freedom of invention. In Felix's literary classes the inmates use their stage names, which sometimes are telling names, sometimes not, but all of them are cryptic, proper prison-slang nicknames: Bent Pencil, Snake-Eye, TimEEz, 8Handz, Leggs, Red Coyote, WonderBoy, PPod, Riceball, and many others.

Another level of the novelist's engagement with language is visible in her explicit use of Shakespeare's text. Atwood's decision to smuggle into her novel a considerable number of Shakespeare's phrases[12] is both bold and risky. On the one hand, it exposes what was the major concern voiced by the critics of the series – that rewriting Shakespeare in modern prose kills the essence of his art. Commenting on the heated discussions among reviewers and readers that followed Hogarth's announcement of the project, Lanier observes that many commentators predicted a failure of the undertaking precisely because the publisher decided to "jettison that most potent signifier of literariness, Shakespeare's language" (2017, 232). Yet, on the other hand, Atwood's own superbly vivid and versatile style, her "gorgeous yet economical prose" (Mandel 2016), is a very friendly environment in which the quotations from *The Tempest* – carefully chosen, never random, used very precisely and always for a special effect and purpose – can be enjoyed, even celebrated. Most of the quotations

---

[12] There are more than a hundred quotations from Shakespeare, including the title and the list of other curses. Most of them are from *The Tempest*, but there are also a few from *Macbeth*, *King Lear*, and *Hamlet*. Most of them are very short – from one word to one line.

are famous lines or phrases, like "the isle is full of noises," "rapt in secret studies" or "high charms," but there are also many others, less significant. Sometimes a single word is used, like "garment" or "usurper," that is not Shakespeare's invention, but is used in the play in a specific and meaningful way. Readers who are well acquainted with the language of the play are thus easily entertained by these reverberations, and it is obvious that Atwood, too, immensely enjoys speaking Shakespeare, or rather, making Shakespeare speak for her purposes.

But Atwood's employment of samples from *The Tempest* is not limited to enhancing the joy of adaptation by introducing textual echoes. It also reflects the novel's power dynamics. It is significant to notice which characters speak Shakespeare most frequently. Felix, of course, who seems to have a proper Shakespearean quote for any occasion. Anne-Marie – less often, but, sharing Felix's profession and being the crucial actress in his production, she is also likely to use Shakespeare's phrases while talking to Felix and to the inmates. Miranda, from time to time, but, because she is the projection of Felix's mind, it may be Felix talking to himself. The inmates speak Shakespeare only within the limits of their roles as students and actors. Notably, characters who know Shakespeare's lines and use them occupy some sort of privileged position, which is meaningful in a literary undertaking whose *raison d'être* is the playwright's cultural capital and which reflects *The Tempest*'s interest in power relations. Significantly, the only other voice to use Shakespeare's phrases as often and as eloquently as Felix belongs to the author herself. As manifested in the way Atwood designed the Contents – all titles of the five sections/acts and most of the chapter titles are quotations from the play– it is the re-teller that is in charge of the artistic charms, who functions as the medium and the distributor of Shakespearean riches. In this way Atwood uses the quotations from the play as another tool to highlight her meta-artistic involvement.

Finally, in Atwood's novel, as in the play, the concern with language is not limited to its artistic uses. Apart from being the tissue of literature and theatre, language is also the tool of education and instruction, of control, as well as of rebellion, on many different levels. In the exposition, Prospero makes his daughter aware of her past by telling the tale that "would cure deafness" (1.2.106),[13] and Atwood designs the first section of her novel, aptly titled "Dark Backward," around an extended retrospection. Miranda teaches Caliban to speak her language, but what she perceives as a benevolent gesture of pity and care is received as an act of oppression and manifestation of power. Caliban's reaction is to use the acquired language selectively in numerous verbal shows of resilience – "my profit on't / Is I know how to curse" (1.2.365–6). Caliban, the master of cursing, is initially the only character of the play whom the inmates see as appealing and relatable, which inspires Felix's first assignment. As an experienced theatrical practitioner turned teacher, Felix knows well that there is no better way of engaging his students with the play than by persuading them to use its language in a way that is natural to them. Cursing is allowed in the classroom, but only with curses taken from the play. As the inmates – having made sure that, as usual, they are playing for cigarettes – bend their heads over the playbooks and scribble the curses industriously into their notebooks, you can almost see Atwood grinning with pleasure as she comments on the prisoners turned philologists, "Your profanity, thinks Felix, has oft been your whoreson hag-born progenitor of literacy" (89). A significant part of Atwood's meta-artistic approach consists in cleverly weaving the language of

---

[13] *The Tempest* is quoted from the Arden Shakespeare edition by Frank Kermode (1958).

her hypotext into her own text in a way that never feels forced and works self-reflexively. The overlapping layers of Shakespeare's language and Atwood's language expose the strengths of both authors and subtly draw the reader's attention to the effectiveness of the art of language.

Another aspect that emerges from the above discussion is that Atwood's meta-artistic perspective manifests itself in the novel's concern with the position of an artist, the significance of artistic creation, and the potentially healing power of art. In Atwood's interpretation, Felix is an alter ego of Prospero, an artist "obsessed with his own genius" (*In Conversation with...* 3:00–3:02). The protagonist's passionate commitment to his job as theatre director clearly parallels Prospero's preference of books and "secret studies" over governing. In both cases the results are detrimental to the character's social and personal life. In both cases, too, the characters, after their downfalls, still depend on what they identify with – the remnants of their powerful art. In her development of the main character, Atwood cleverly supplies conflicting signals that shape the reader's ambiguous response. One may pity Felix and therefore justify his workaholism as an attempt to deal with his wife's death. Moreover, one can easily accept his engrossment in theatre because of the stereotypical perception of artists as unconditionally devoted to their artistic vocation. But Atwood also makes sure that, at the same time, one is repulsed by Felix's self-pity, egotism, hubris and bitterness. Like Prospero, Felix is not a likeable person, but he is definitely a master of his art. There is nothing he knows and understands better than theatre and it is clear that this knowledge helps him to manipulate his students and mould them into actors. But, although the power dynamics in the prison classes are naturally shaped by Felix's privileged position, Atwood ensures that the inmates-turned-actors are granted some opportunities to slide out of his control. They actively create their roles, rewrite the play-text and negotiate Felix's interpretations. Artistic creation – even if limited and practised occasionally – becomes for them a means of expression, a sphere of temporary independence and a form of protest when, conducted by their teacher/director, they use theatrical illusion to oppose the administrative decisions of soulless governing institutions and save the prison literacy programme.

It has to be admitted that Atwood's resolution has been rightly criticised as naïve and unrealistic.[14] She is silent about the predictably dire consequences of the prison *coup*. After all, the inmates' "engagement in the performance-turned-riot seems to negate the transformative effect of the theatrical workshop (...) [b]y helping Felix undergo his own transformation, they are, in fact, returning to their previous criminal identities" (Bartnicka 2021, 32). Are we to believe that the repentant ministers cover up the whole matter and all live happily ever after? Perhaps we are; after all, the literacy programme is to be continued and the inmates have plans to stage their own play on Caliban. The ending is perhaps too easy, definitely brighter and more hopeful than Shakespeare's. Atwood risks a lot, but she is remarkably consistent in the ways she develops the theme of isolation and imprisonment picked up from *The Tempest* and modulated in her own way.

---

[14] E.g., Emily St. John Mandel in her review for The New York Times writes that "the prison production of *The Tempest* leads to some of the book's clunkiest elements. At least some of the prisoners are in on Felix's plot. (...) These are inmates in a medium-security prison, who are being asked to menace two federal ministers. They've been told the literacy program is in peril, but this alone can't explain why they'd risk longer sentences, deferred parole or transfer to maximum security for such a harebrained scheme" (Mandel 2016). It is true that in terms of probability Atwood is walking on thin ice, but I would say that, at the risk of operating on the verge of veracity, she locates herself close to the position of a magician, one who controls things inexplicable by reason, and this is part of the rules of the game she is playing with *The Tempest*.

The novelist admits in an interview that what led her to the idea of setting her retelling in a prison was Prospero's pleading in the final line of his epilogue: "set me free" (*Margaret Atwood retells Shakespeare...*). In fact, the play's epilogue contains as many as six phrases referring to imprisonment and releasing: "I must be here confined by you," "Let me not, / (...) dwell / in this bare island by your spell; / But release me from my bands," "my ending is despair, / Unless I be relieved by prayer, / Which (...) / frees all faults," "Let your indulgence set me free" (Epilogue 4–20). While certainly being a conventional meta-theatrical finale, the ultimate aside Shakespeare's audiences would await as encouragement to applaud the players, the epilogue recapitulates the play's central themes of freedom, confinement, servitude, and forgiveness. Inspired by these words, the novelist makes her protagonist rely on the prisons depicted and suggested in the play in an attempt to find a key that might bring this play closer to his inmate students who are understandably discouraged by the magic, fairies, masques and lack of realistic happenings. Felix feels like a prisoner, too. Inspecting his prison classroom and rehearsal place he cannot but think: "My island domain. My place of exile. My penance. My theatre" (81). As their second assignment, his students count all the play's prisons and jailers to later work on the staging with these situations of confinement in mind. Guided by the prisons of the play, the inmate actors deal with their traumas by investigating the limits of freedom, the restrictions of confinement, and the invigorating perspective of release.[15]

The numerous situations of confinement that Atwood weaves into her rewriting are enriched by one more, not mentioned explicitly, but

---

[15] Commenting on the complex relations in the novel between freedom and creativity, Nishevita Jayendran observes that the creative acts presented "also create prisons until other creative retellings set them free. Herein lies one point of convergence of freedom, discursive spaces and the politics of creativity, in literature and culture" (2020).

one that her intertextual interactions with *The Tempest* brings into focus. It is actually a double imprisonment. Felix, imprisoned in his unprocessed grief throughout all the years, keeps Miranda prisoner by insisting on her ghostly presence in his life. The final relief in Felix's grief, the moment when his prolonged mourning can finally be over, is the realisation that comes to him at the very end of the novel, at the end of a process which subtly reflects Prospero's transformation. He becomes aware that, on the day of Miranda's funeral, he virtually took his daughter prisoner by refusing to accept her death: "She couldn't have simply vanished from the universe. He'd refused to believe that" (15). Shakespeare's play traces the process of Prospero's transformation from an angry revenger to a forgiving brother and the restorer of peace, ready to come back to the real world of politics, even if he has to accommodate the risks resulting from only partly successful correction and rather unconvincing reconciliation. It is debatable whether he does so for the sake of Miranda's happy future, in an attempt to secure a political alliance, or in order to sustain his parental immortality project,[16] but his surviving daughter is of key importance no matter what motivates him. By making Felix's Miranda die at the age of three, Atwood complicates the situation by making the psychological portrayal of her protagonist more complex and the appeal of his plight more universal, relying on common human experience of loss and bereavement. In this way her retelling becomes a study of incomplete grief with its obsessively recurring images of the lost daughter and equally obsessive attachment to *The Tempest*. This is one more level on which one can note Atwood's meta-artistic concerns. Approaching the novel

---

[16] For a discussion of *The Tempest* in the context of death-denying projects, see: Calderwood 1987, 187–194.

from the perspective of trauma studies, Paul Joseph Zajac argues that Atwood "exposes a resemblance between these forms of repetition related to trauma and the process of adapting a (...) text, which Linda Hutcheon defines as 'repetition without replication'" (2020, 325). "Shakespeare provides a script by which Felix can communicate his bereavement" (2020, 329), when "[b]y assuming the role of Prospero – or being possessed by it – Felix rehearses and rehashes his suffering" (2020, 332).

In its initial stages, Felix tries to process his grief via the artistic attempt to revive Miranda in his staging – "after the funeral with its pathetically small coffin he'd plunged himself into *The Tempest*. It was an evasion, (...) but it was also to be a kind of reincarnation" (15). When the preparations were stopped by Tony's betrayal, the processing of grief was left incomplete, giving rise to hatred, vengefulness, and the gradual aggravation of Felix's mental condition. This is the second time he imprisons himself in grief, not letting Miranda go again and, instead, forcing her to accompany him in the ambiguous status of an imaginary companion. The realisation of his mistake, expressed in the novel's epilogue, "comes over him in a wave: he's been wrong about his *Tempest*, wrong for twelve years. The endgame of his obsession wasn't to bring his Miranda back to life. The endgame was something quite different" (283). It was to release her. In her meta-artistic literary game Atwood seems to be suggesting that, as Prospero needed his masque to realise that even the most spectacular illusions cannot set him and his daughter free, so Felix needed to complete his artistic undertaking in order to cleanse himself from the detrimental, and confining, influence of prolonged grief. Allowing Felix to free himself from grief by releasing Miranda, Atwood makes her epilogue richer, more conclusive and more hopeful in comparison to Shakespeare's. Two major confinements are abandoned. Some readers may see this as too sentimental and disappointingly flattening *The Tempest*'s bittersweet conclusion, but most of them would allow the cathartic emotions to overwhelm them.[17]

Last but not least, Felix's third assignment is yet another meta-artistic gesture Atwood includes in her novel. It is an allusion to the centuries-long reception of the play that produced so many different versions and continuations. All the five teams of actors gathered around their character – Ariel, Evil Bro Antonio, Miranda, Gonzalo, and Hag-Seed – "were supposed to figure out what happens to [their] team's main guy after the end of the play" (247). And so they did, very inventively and with full engagement, which resulted, in some cases, in separate mini performances illustrating the character's imagined extratextual future. Symptomatically, Team Hag-Seed proposed the most spectacular, eloquent and thorough "afterlife" for their character's future. It is Hag-Seed that the inmates feel most related to and sympathise with, so they are all "listening intently: they really care what happens to Caliban" (264). Not only does Caliban turn out to be Prospero's son, but Prospero's words "this thing of darkness I / Acknowledge mine" (5.1.275–6) are taken to signify his recognition of this fact and his later actions are undertaken to atone for the previous abandonment and neglect of Caliban and his mother. Shakespeare's Caliban is sensitive to music, so Team Hag-Seed endow their character with a full-scale musical talent. After Prospero takes him to Milan, he uses his second chance and, with his father's help, becomes a famous musician. "He can bring out, like, the darkness emotions in people, but in a musical way. He was to keep away from booze though (...) he makes the effort, and he stays clean. (...) Prospero's really proud of him" (267). If with this somewhat naïve picture of Caliban's future

---

[17] Cf., e.g., some of the reviews quoted in the blurb.

Atwood balances on the verge of sentimentality, it is thoroughly consistent with the novel's overall emphasis on the theme of redemption.[18] Leggs and his team are even imagining a new play, independent of *The Tempest*, that would focus entirely on Caliban's freeing himself from his slave/servant status, an idea which makes Felix observe that "Caliban has escaped the play. (...) Now there's no one to restrain him" (272). If, following Lanier's suggestion, "we identify Prospero with Shakespeare the author-function, Felix's line aptly describes the enterprise of retelling Shakespeare itself" (2017, 245).

The culmination of Atwood's meta-artistic engagement with *The Tempest* can be seen in the position of the play's summary. Placing her summary at the end of the retelling, Atwood creates a space for yet another level of the Shakespearean game. As has been argued by Muñoz-Valdivieso,

> Atwood's ending seems to be a playful wink to her devoted readers to apply their own magic in their response to this quirky, multifaceted, hag-seed of a novel which both is and is not *The Tempest*—a peculiar polymorphic creature that (...) is the offspring of two magicians: Shakespeare and Atwood, Atwood and Shakespeare. (2017, 126)

If this is to be seen as an act of communication with the novelist's readers, it can be understood in various ways. It is a reminder about the nature of adaptation, one that without any complexes titles the summary "*The Tempest*: The Original." It encourages readers to plunge into Shakespeare's play-text, perhaps for the first time, and to go on

---

[18] On the persistent presence of the theme of redemption in this and other Hogarth Shakespeare novels, see: Lanier 2017, 243–247.

for themselves, relying on their imagination and interpretative instincts, now that the example has been set by the novelist herself. It also reflects the publisher's intentions to bring the Shakespearean playwrighting heritage closer to contemporary readers by offering the retelling as a kind of bridge leading towards the play, rather than – if the summary had preceded the novel – suggesting the play's inspirational potential only. Last but not least, Atwood reminds us that it is her own expertise on how to use the textual bricks to create this bridge, that it is her writing art that has guided us through the maze of the intertextual interactions, and that she is confident enough to offer her retelling as a self-standing literary entertainment *vis à vis* Shakespeare's canonical text.

Atwoodian Shakespeare and Shakespearean Atwood: A conclusion

At the beginning of this chapter I summarised the publisher's purposes and objectives behind the Hogarth Shakespeare's project – the ambitious, though somewhat risky, endeavour which granted the novelists a considerable amount of freedom to create their own stories, but in such a way that the plays they would retell were easily recognisable. The Shakespearean Atwood, *Hag-Seed*, perhaps the most successful novel in the series, is

> a beautifully constructed adaptation, one that stands on its own but is even richer when read against its source – and can, in turn, enrich its source material. It's playful and thoughtful, and it singlehandedly makes a good argument for the value of adapting Shakespeare. (Grady 2016)

For many readers, one of the novel's advantages is the fact that it "feels so much like something Atwood would have written anyway" (Groskop 2016). Atwood's critics and fans alike can easily recognize in this book interests, techniques and devices that can be described as typical of her writing (cf.: Percec 2018; Kuester 2019; Jayendran 2020; Livingstone 2022). Yet, according to some of the novel's recipients, one aspect makes this Shakespeare not Atwoodian enough. It has been claimed that, "somewhat surprisingly, given Atwood's reputation as a feminist" (Danebrock 2021, 113), the novelist has withdrawn from her usual perspective on the function and agency of female characters.

In her book on women novelists appropriating Shakespeare, Sanders observes that these writers, "products of particular times and moments in the history of Shakespeare's studies," "are often engaging with the critical and historical reception of the playwright and his world as much as with subjective interpretation" (2001, 12). While Atwood's choice of *The Tempest* might have suggested the writer's intention to engage with the topics of farther-daughter relationship and/or patriarchy (cf. Sanders 2001, 5), to the disappointment of some readers, the novel can hardly be described as feminist. Ignoring Sycorax and Claribel, reducing Miranda to "a rather dutiful housewife" (Danebrock 2021, 118), showing Anne-Marie as Felix's "adoptive" daughter (Danebrock 2021, 117), and under-developing the character of Estella, "[w]ith practically an all male cast in both the novel and the play, Atwood seems to barely touch on feminist concerns" (Livingstone 2022, 94).[19]

The reasons for Atwood's lack of involvement in feminist concerns may be connected with the project's generally traditionalist approach.

---

[19] David Livingstone nevertheless agrees with Atwood defending a writer's "right to creative freedom, regardless of people's expectations" (2022, 96).

The Hogarth Shakespeare was criticised for being "fairly conservative in its reiteration of a humanist idea of selfhood, its modernist exploration of consciousness, and its return to the conventional (or commonsensical) understanding of Shakespearean character" (Schülting 2020, 45) and uninterested in "the political and cultural issues of our day" (Livingstone 2022, 91). Yet I am more inclined to see it as a consequence of a deliberate decision to focus on the exploration of the meta-artistic potential that the rewriting commissioned by the publisher encouraged.

Atwood is apparently ready to acknowledge that there seems to be no limit to the cultural multiplication of such meta-artistic games. Soon after *Hag-Seed* had been published, she was requested by an actual theatre tutor working in prisons for permission to turn her novel into a play about a person putting on a play in prison (*In Conversation with...* 5:35–6:14). If adaptation is "a creative and interpretive transposition of a recognisable other work," "a kind of extended palimpsest" (Hutcheon 2006, 33), Atwood enthusiastically engages her creative powers in contributing to these palimpsestic transformations.

References

Atwood, Margaret. 2002. *Negotiating with the Dead: A Writer on Writing*. Cambridge. Cambridge University Press.

Atwood, Margaret. 2016a. "A Perfect Storm: Margaret Atwood on Rewriting *The Tempest*." *The Guardian* September 24. https://www.theguardian.com/books/2016/sep/24/margaret-atwood-rewriting-shakespeare-tempest-hag-seed (accessed 10 September 2023).

Atwood, Margaret. 2016b. *Hag-Seed. "The Tempest" Retold*. London. Penguin Random House.

Auden, Wystan Hugh. 2002. *Lectures on Shakespeare*. Ed. Arthur Kirsch. Princeton and Oxford. Princeton University Press.

Bartnicka, Anna Joanna. 2021. "Margaret Atwood's *Hag-Seed*: Dramatic Encounters between Classic and Adaptation, Life and Art, Freedom and Imprisonment." *Roczniki Humanistyczne* LXIX(11), 21–33.

Bloom, Harold. 1997. *The Anxiety of Influence. A Theory of Poetry*. New York and Oxford. Oxford University Press.

Calderwood, James L. 1987. *Shakespeare and the Denial of Death*. Amherst. University of Massachusetts Press.

Danebrock, Friederike. 2021. "The Ninth Prison. Desert Islands and no Witch in Margaret Atwood's *Hag-Seed*." *Australian Studies Journal* 35, 111–125.

Dobson, Michael and Stanley Wells, eds. 2001. *The Oxford Companion to Shakespeare*. Oxford. Oxford University Press.

Genette, Gérard. 1997. *Palimpsests. Literature in the Second Degree*. Translated by Channa Newsman and Claude Doubinsky. Lincoln, NE. University of Nebraska Press.

Grady, Constance. 2016. "Margaret Atwood's New Book *Hag-Seed* Proves the Value of Adapting Shakespeare." https://www.vox.com/culture/2016/10/13/13231678/hag-seed-margaret-atwood-review (accessed 31 July 2023).

Groskop, Viv. 2016. "*Hag-Seed* Review – Margaret Atwood Turns *The Tempest* into a Perfect Storm." *The Guardian* 16 October 2016. https://www.theguardian.com/books/2016/oct/16/hag-seed-review-margaret-atwood-tempest-hogarth-shakespeare (accessed 11 September 2023).

Hogarth. https://www.penguin.co.uk/company/publishers/vintage/hogarth (accessed 10 October 2023).

Hutcheon, Linda. 2006. *A Theory of Adaptation*. London and New York. Routledge.

In Conversation with Margaret Atwood on "The Tempest." 2018. https://www.youtube.com/watch?v=nQ3-dqxRT2Y (accessed 20 October 2023).

Jayendran, Nishevita. 2020. "'Set Me Free': Spaces and the Politics of Creativity in Margaret Atwood's *Hag-Seed*." *Journal of Language, Literature and Culture* 67(1), 15–27.

Kubińska, Olga and Ewa Nawrocka, eds. 2004. *Playing Games with Shakespeare. Contemporary Reception of Shakespeare in the Baltic Region*. Gdańsk. Theatrum Gedanense Fundation.

Kuester, Martin. 2019. "Shakespearean Godgames in Makeshiweg, Ont.: Margaret Atwood's *Hag-Seed* (2016)." In: *The Anglo-Canadian Novel in the Twenty-First Century: Interpretations*. Eds. Maria Löschnigg and Martin Löschnigg. Heidelberg. Winter Verlag, 33–41.

Lanier, Douglas M. 2017. "The Hogarth Shakespeare Series: Redeeming Shakespeare's Literariness." In: *Shakespeare and Millennial Fiction*. Ed. Andrew James Hartley. Cambridge. Cambridge University Press, 230–250.

Lindley, David. 2002. *Introduction*. In: William Shakespeare, *The Tempest*. Ed. David Lindley. Cambridge. Cambridge University Press, 1–83.

Livingstone, David. 2022. "Insubstantial Pageant: Adapting Shakespeare in Two Texts from the Hogarth Shakespeare Project." *Hradec Králové Journal of Anglophone Studies* 9(1–2), 90–98.

Mandel, Emily St. John. 2016. "Margaret Atwood Meets Shakespeare in a Retelling of *The Tempest*." *The New York Times*. https://www.nytimes.com/2016/10/30/books/review/hag-seed-tempest-retold-margaret-atwood.html (accessed 16 April 2023).

Margaret Atwood Retells Shakespeare Play in New Book "Hag-Seed." 2016. The Canadian Press. https://www.youtube.com/watch?v=2qJpL5cWVFE (accessed 20 July 2023).

Muñoz-Valdivieso, Sofía. 2017. "Shakespeare Our Contemporary in 2016: Margaret Atwood's Rewriting of *The Tempest* in *Hag-Seed*." *SEDERI* 27, 105–129.

Percec, Dana. 2018. "The Canadian Tempest. Margaret Atwood and Shakespeare Retold as *Hag-Seed*." *Caietele Echinox* 34. Posthumanist Configurations, 295–307.

Sanders, Julie. 2001. *Novel Shakespeares. Twentieth-Century Women Novelists and Appropriation*. Manchester and New York. Manchester University Press.

Sanders, Julie. 2006. *Adaptation and Appropriation*. London. Routledge.

Schülting, Sabine. 2020. "Tales (not) from Shakespeare: Shakespeare 'Re-told' for the 21st Century." *And Thereby Hangs a Tale: A Critical Anatomy of (Popular)*

Tales. Eds. Ina Habermann and Christian Krug. Erlangen. FAU University Press, 37–53.

Shakespeare, William. 1958. *The Tempest*. The Arden Shakespeare. Ed. Frank Kermode. Cambridge, Mass. Harvard University Press.

Shakespeare, William. 1999. *The Tempest*. The Arden Shakespeare. Eds. Virginia Mason Vaughan and Alden T. Vaughan. Walton-on-Thames, Surrey. Thomas Nelson and Sons.

Tatar, Yağmur. 2020. "'Spirits to Enforce, Art to Enchant': Metatheatricality and Art in *The Tempest* and *Hag-seed*." *B.A.S. British and American Studies* XXVI, 93–100.

Vaughan, Virginia Mason. 2009. "Literary Invocations of *The Tempest*." In: *The Cambridge Companion to Shakespeare's Last Plays*. Ed. Catherine M. S. Alexander. Cambridge. Cambridge University Press.

Vaughan, Virginia Mason and Alden T. Vaughan. 1999. *Introduction*. In: William Shakespeare, *The Tempest*. Eds. Virginia Mason Vaughan and Alden T. Vaughan. Bristol. ITP Arden Shakespeare, 1–138.

Voigts, Eckart. 2014. "A Theatre of Attraction: Colonialism, Gender; and The Tempest's Performance History." In: *The Tempest. A Critical Reader*. Eds. Alden T. Vaughan and Virginia Mason Vaughan. London and New York. Bloomsbury Arden Shakespeare, 39–60.

Zajac, Paul Joseph. 2020. "Prisoners of Shakespeare: Trauma and Adaptation in Atwood's *Hag-Seed*." *Studies in the Novel* 52(3), 324–343.

Index

Abdalkafor Ola 39
Agamben Giorgio ix, 2, 10–14, 38
Alhashmi Rawad 37, 45
Allen Graham 43
Arendt Hannah 15, 54
Atwood Margaret x, 96, 97, 99–103,
      105, 106, 108, 109, 111,
      112, 115–120
Aubyn Edward St. 97
Auden W. H. 93, 94, 95
Austen Jane 99
Ayers John W. 61
Bahoora Haytham 37, 38
Banerjee Debjani 21
Bartnicka Anna Joanna 112
Begum Shamima 16, 17
Benjamin Walter 13
Bloom Harold 97
Booker M. Keith 40, 41, 42, 55
Boulos Edward 35

Browning Robert 95
Burton Robert 67
Butler Judith ix, x, 4–7, 9, 10
Calderwood James 114
Campbell Denis 61
Cantor Pul A. 84
Carson Anne 2
Chambers Claire 19
Chevalier Tracy 97
Choudhury Tufyal 15, 17
Clark Anne 48, 49
Cottom Daniel 33
Crawford Nicolas 70, 72
Cribb T.J. 69
Danebrock Friederike 119
Daniel Drew 62
Daraiseh Isra 40, 41, 42, 55
Davenant William 94
Dessen Alan 68
Doolittle Hilda 95

Index

Dryden John 94
Duignan Brian 54
Eagleton Terry 28
Eliasson Albin 48
Fargues Émilien 14, 16
Fernie Ewan 70
Fitzmaurice Andrew 81
Flynn Ged 61
Frank Michael C. 18
Frankenstein Victor ix, 33, 41, 47, 48
Genette Gérard 43, 103
Githens-Mazer Jonathan 18, 19
Godwin William vii, viii
Goethe Johan Wolfgang von 6
Goldhill Simon 24
Gouge William 59
Grady Constance 118
Grady Hugh 69, 70
Groskop Viv 99, 119
Heaney Seamus 2, 3, 6, 7
Hegel Georg Wilhelm Friedrich 4, 70
Henick Mark 60
Heriyanto Devina 19
Hiliyard Paddy 17
Honig Bonnie 6, 7, 8, 23
Hutcheon Linda 98, 115, 120
Jacobson Howard 97
Javid Sajid 16
Jayendran Nishevita 113, 119
Jebb R.C. 6
Kahn Coppélia 69
Kakutani Michiko 54

Kermode Frank 110
Kingston Lindsey N. 14, 15
Kirkpatrick Jennet 23
Kitto H.D.F. 6
Kleiner John 70
Kottman Paul A. 70
Krause Peter 2
Kristeva Julia 69
Kubińska Olga 96
Kuester Martin 101, 119
Kwiatek Anna x
Lacan Jacques 4, 5
Langley Eric 62
Lanier Douglas M. 97, 98, 105
Laurence Friar 65, 66, 73, 74
Laurence Margaret 95
Lauriola Rosanna 9
Leonard Miriam 5, 7
Levenson Jill L. 65, 69
Lindley David 93
Livingstone David 119, 120
Lynch Orla 18
MacDonald Michael 76, 79
Macfie Pamela 77
MacKaye Percy 95
Mandel Emily St. John 108, 112
Master Mercedes 16
McLuskie Kathleen E. 69
Meltzer Françoise 5
Mendoza Kirsten 63
Millais John Everett 89
Muñoz-Valdivieso Sofia 99, 102, 117

Murphy Sinéad 37, 40
Naqvi Zainab Batu 15, 17, 18
Nawrocka Ewa 96
Naylor Gloria 95
Nesbo Jo 97
Niederktotenthaler Thomas 61
O'Neill Stephen 63
Percec Dana 99, 100, 119
Połczyńska Marcelina ix
Price Anthony 101
Regilme Salvador 16
Robert William 5
Romanowska Agnieszka xi
Saadawi Ahmed ix, 34, 35, 37-39,
　　41, 42, 44, 45, 47, 49-51,
　　53-55
Sanders Julie 99
Schülting Sabine 120
Shadwell Thomas 94
Shakespeare William viii, ix, x, 62, 63,
　　67, 69, 70, 78, 84, 87, 88, 89,
　　93-100, 102, 105, 106, 108,
　　109, 113, 114, 117, 118
Shamsie Kamila viii, 1, 2, 14, 16, 19,
　　20, 22, 25, 27, 28
Shelley Mary vii, viii, ix, 33, 34, 41,
　　47, 55

Smith Philip x
Snyder Susan 70
Sobolewska Maria 18
Solon 8
Sophocles viii, 5, 19, 24
Sym John 59
Tatar Yağmur 100, 101
Tronicke Marlena 62, 71, 76
Tyler Anne 97
Vargo Lisa vii, viii, 33
Vaughan Alden T. 94, 105
Vaughan Virginia Mason 94, 95, 96, 105
Voigts Eckart 94
Walton Robert 47, 48, 49
Warner Marina 95
Watchman Chief 74
Wawrzyńczyk Wiktoria ix
Webber Frances 15, 16
Weiss Naomi 2
Wells 93
Williams Zoe 60
Wiltshire Susan Ford 8
Winterson Jeanette 97
Woolf Leonard 97
Woolf Virginia 97
Wymer Rowland 62, 70, 84
Zajac Paul Joseph 114

Managing editor
Zofia Sajdek

Language editor
Martyna Ogórek

Proofreading
Klaudia Król-Kiełbowicz

Typesetting
Paweł Noszkiewicz

Jagiellonian University Press
Editorial Offices: Michałowskiego 9/2, 31-126 Kraków, Poland
Phone: +48 12 663 23 80

GPSR Authorized Representative: Easy Access System Europe, Mustamäe tee
50, 10621 Tallinn, Estonia, gpsr.requests@easproject.com

www.ingramcontent.com/pod-product-compliance
Lightning Source LLC
Jackson TN
JSHW012303190325
81101JS00018B/61